T0164902

The Spiritual Hedonista's 9 Ingredients for Delicious Living

The Spiritual Hedonista's 9 Ingredients for Delicious Living

Reflections on the Teachings of Abraham

Amélie Eden

BALBOA.
PRESS
A DIVISION OF HAY HOUSE

Copyright © 2012 Amélie Eden

All rights reserved. No part of this book may be used or reproduced by
any means, graphic, electronic, or mechanical, including photocopying,
recording, taping or by any information storage retrieval system
without the written permission of the publisher except in the case
of brief quotations embodied in critical articles and reviews.

Balboa Press books may be ordered through booksellers or by contacting:

Balboa Press
A Division of Hay House
1663 Liberty Drive
Bloomington, IN 47403
www.balboapress.com
1-(877) 407-4847

Because of the dynamic nature of the Internet, any web addresses or
links contained in this book may have changed since publication and
may no longer be valid. The views expressed in this work are solely those
of the author and do not necessarily reflect the views of the publisher,
and the publisher hereby disclaims any responsibility for them.

The author of this book does not dispense medical advice or prescribe the use
of any technique as a form of treatment for physical, emotional, or medical
problems without the advice of a physician, either directly or indirectly. The
intent of the author is only to offer information of a general nature to help
you in your quest for emotional and spiritual well-being. In the event you use
any of the information in this book for yourself, which is your constitutional
right, the author and the publisher assume no responsibility for your actions.

Any people depicted in stock imagery provided by Thinkstock are models,
and such images are being used for illustrative purposes only.
Certain stock imagery © Thinkstock.

ISBN: 978-1-4525-4846-3 (sc)
ISBN: 978-1-4525-4847-0 (e)

Printed in the United States of America

Balboa Press rev. date: 3/27/2012

For My Beautiful Mozart- You are the embodiment of grace, beauty, discernment, unconditional love and connection to Source Energy. I will always love You.

Contents

Acknowledgements

First and Foremost, I would like to thank the teachers who have influenced my life the most in the deepest and most profound ways. The first teacher I would like to thank is Louise Hay, who has taught me that I can heal my life, and ever since I picked up her book when I was 9 years old and embarked on my Spiritual Path, I have healed my life on every level possible and continue on to do so. Secondly, I would like to thank Esther and Jerry Hicks along with Abraham, teachers who have brought an endless and infinite amount of joy and comfort into my life on a daily basis. Your teachings are the miracles I have sought for a lifetime and are the pure inspiration for this book.

I would also like to thank all of the brilliant and beautiful artists in this world who have provided me with endless inspiration and joy through my simple gaze upon the gorgeousness of their work. The countless artists in French cinema, French painters, Spanish painters, amazing European architects, talented landscapers, and last but not least, the delightful spinners of words who have inspired me to activate my own inner Mozart.

Lastly, I would like to thank all of those souls who inspired me to grow into the person who I am today and the person who I am evolving to be. These are the people with whom I have disagreed with, argued with, or even fought with. These rascals helped me to confirm with myself Who I Really Am and Who I Want to Be, and for that I am forever grateful.

Preface

It is with great pleasure that I write the preface for the first book in the *Spiritual Hedonista* series. It is written from the point of view of my Higher Self, the part of me that is connected to Source Energy and all that is. This book focuses on 9 principles that have worked for me throughout my life in order to bring me more joy, pleasure, and happiness. They are principles which I can personally vouch for, rely upon, and take pleasure in sharing.

I have gone through my own fair share of traumas and troubles in life as does most anyone on this planet, although most would consider my experiences to fall on the more dramatic end. Regardless of what I or anyone else has been through, we can all start to live a better life from right where we are, no matter where that place is. That last statement is something that I have repeated to myself many times throughout my life and one which has worked for me. It has helped me to move through my own self-doubt, insecurities, anxieties, and uncertainties. It does not matter when you decide to change your life, as age is just a number given perceptual value by human beings. And problems are perceptual as well: challenges that are temporary, transient experiences that all serve in our personal growth and expansion. It doesn't matter where you are today, because what matters is where you are going and how you feel.

The greatest teachings that I have received to date are the lessons I have learned from Abraham who has taught millions of people around the world that, "nothing is more important than that you feel good." What a very simple yet deeply profound lesson, and one that has served me and led me to writing this book. Abraham's teachings changed my life forever. Although I consider myself to have been on my spiritual path consciously by the age of 7, and then assuredly by the time I was ripe young age of 9, I still had so many unanswered questions about life swirling around within my inner being. Abraham filled in all of the blanks for me and answered those questions. And the reason why I knew that those answers were right is because they made the most clear, logical sense out of anything that I have read and experienced thus far.

With dedication and persistence, I delved into the Abraham teachings. I had been reading spiritual books since I was 9 years old, studied the teachings of various religions, and it wasn't until decades later that I began my Abraham experience, at just the right time. The most important piece of knowledge that Abraham teaches is the power of feeling good, which is the most important part of all of life. However, this lesson is the one component in most Spiritual teachings that I have studied thus far which seems to be missing in a big way.

As I reflected upon this power of feeling good and the power of what Abraham calls, "moving up the emotional scale", my life has gotten better and better. Some old and unhealthy relationships which I had been holding onto fell away, as did many old beliefs, circumstances, and events which no longer served me in the positive direction that I was headed.

My life was good in so many ways before I met Abraham, but after Abraham my life went to a whole other level. It is from this place where I have written this book and continue this dialogue with you. I can tell you from personal experience that these teachings work in a gradual, yet magical way. I write today from a place of excellent health, a pure state of joy, experiencing more prosperity than I ever have in my life thus far, and enjoying a peace and calm that is unlike anything I have ever experienced. I have moved from being a person with some control issues who often felt mistrustful of others, to a person who trusts the Universe at a very deep level. And while it took me a while to get to where I am, the journey was wonderful, clarifying, and continues to be so in an ever expansive way.

So, why is this book called, *The Spiritual Hedonista's 9 Ingredients for Delicious Living*? As Osho, the famous Indian spiritual teacher expresses in his book, *I Say Unto You, Volume 2*, there is a hedonism which is spiritual and divine, going beyond the mere pleasures of the physical body, which he refers to this as spiritual hedonism, or divine hedonism. He also refers to this as being a higher hedonism, as opposed to a lower hedonism which is solely focused upon physical pleasures. This higher hedonism is what he describes as 'living life from the soul.' This is the hedonism to which I refer to in this book. It is a spiritual hedonism, in which I teach from a place of experiencing my physical body through what Abraham often refers to as 'through the eyes of Source'.

My wish for you is to take from this book that which works for you and feels good to you. It is my wish that you trust yourself more, appreciate yourself more, and love yourself more. And it is also my wish that you let go of all that you hold onto which holds you back, for you deserve all of the magic of the Universe that is waiting to fall at your feet.

With Love,

Amélie Eden

Introduction

When you see your world through the eyes of your Divine and total Self, even breathing can be a delicious and pleasurable experience...

One of the greatest teachings of Abraham is how one can move from where they are to the place where they can see the world through the eyes of their highest self- Source Energy, as they refer to it. Seeing the world through these eyes changes everything: one's life circumstances, events, and manifestations. This connection with one's spirit or soul is what makes physical life so delicious. To live a physical experience with complete connection to Source is the basis for all of the sweetness of life. It is the joy and the pleasure that we all seek. It is like living in pleasure each and every day. Living life in this way can be referred to as Spiritual Hedonism.

So what exactly is Spiritual Hedonism, and what exactly can I learn from the Spiritual Hedonista about life, let alone, how to live life deliciously? Well, if you are reading this book, it is very unlikely that you would need further explanation about the word *spiritual*. In fact, you have probably come to your own conclusions about what that word means, and whatever you have come to conclude, you are right. However, the word *hedonista* requires further explanation. The word *hedonista* is the Spanish word for hedonist. And in this particular case, describing a hedonist in a feminine form. However, further explanation of the word hedonist is warranted, especially since the word has developed a bad reputation over time.

A hedonist is simply one who lives for pleasure or is a pleasure seeker. How this word over time became one which indicates perversion, excessiveness, or immorality is a phenomena which has been misguided, and the use of the word *hedonist* has been misdirected. Oftentimes society tends to focus on the negative side of a subject, amplify it, and dramatize it for effect. And while it is quite obvious by observing society that there are many people who use the word hedonist to mask or justify things such as addictions, sexual perversions, or anything that society considers undesirable behaviour, the pure literal sense of the word is a person who lives for pleasure and consistently seeks it. And while an individual's personal sense of pleasure is relative, the literal meaning of hedonism can include both what society deems to be acceptable and unacceptable. This book however is not interested in morality nor does it address it, but it is interested in helping people to feel better and to feel good, through means that are physically and personally beneficial, legal, and available to all regardless of financial or personal circumstance. This books aims to help one to feel better first and foremost in his or her mind, which is the most important and the solely important place to feel good. For if you feel good in your mind, then everything physical on the outside follows suit. And no matter what you consider to be pleasure or pleasurable, as with the natural change and flow of life, those current ideas of yours are likely to change, and that's okay.

There have been numerous schools of thought created throughout history regarding pleasure seeking, the right way to do it, the wrong way to do it, and the psychoanalysis behind all of it. Sigmund Freud, the famous psychoanalyst, created the theories of the *Pleasure Principle* and the *Reality Principle* which basically states that humans seek pleasure and avoid circumstances of pain. As they get older and are socialized, they learn about the necessity to delay pleasure (the *Reality Principle*) and not to be fixated on instant gratification as most children are (and some adults you may know). While all of these teachings have great value to many and have served great importance to the masses, this book is addressing Spiritual Hedonism in the present day, from a whole new, modern-day perspective. While there really is not a right or wrong way to use this term, it is important to clarify the context in which it is being used in this book so that everyone is on the same page so to speak.

OK, Spiritual Hedonista, what do YOU mean by Spiritual Hedonism?

One might ask, "How can spirituality and hedonism relate to each other, let alone be combined into one term? The two words seem to be somewhat contradictory." To answer that question, it is first best to address the term 'pleasure'. Pleasure comes in many forms. However, through misguided media, the focus upon hedonism has been placed upon pleasure seeking through negative, harmful, or self-destructive means such as through sex addiction and endless encounters of unprotected sex, drug addiction, and food addiction. These addictions can be associated with activities which some might consider pleasurable, but pleasure which is attached to pain is not the type of pleasure addressed in this book. The types of addictions just mentioned all have pain attached to them. They are associated with a pleasurable instant gratification, shortly followed by the pain of the dissipation of the pleasure. It is a pleasure-pain cycle which this book does not address, nor does it condemn, for Source Energy does not condemn one's choices but merely observes. While there are substances and lifestyles that bring instant gratification but destruction to health or relationships, this book addresses the large arena of the human experience that can be pleasurable *and* can be healthy, enlightening, creative, uplifting, and long-lasting, going far beyond the level of instant gratification. It is to these types of pleasures that this book focuses upon: pleasures which are free from pain, addiction, or negative emotion. They are pleasures experienced through connection with Source Energy.

An example of this is cooking delicious meals for yourself, for loved ones, or for customers, if you are in the culinary arts industry. This can be a healthy and wonderful form of pleasure which can be passed down as an art form for generations. This is a form of hedonism which has inspired the world famous food magazine, *Epicurious*, named after the Greek philosopher, *Epicurus*, who developed his own ideas about pleasure seeking and hedonism. He is the founder of the philosophy of *Epicureanism*, which advocated happiness, self-sufficiency, peace, tranquillity, a life surrounded by friends, and freedom from fear and pain. He taught that what is good is pleasurable and what is bad is painful. While Epicurus has been seen to be a great teacher throughout time about hedonism, even many years after his death, the Spiritual Hedonista approach is to encourage people to be their own greatest teacher about what it is to live a pleasurable life. The Spiritual Hedonista approach is to be your own guru by following your own inner guidance, a teaching of Abraham, and one that is one of the most effective teachings available to date. This book speaks to the part of You that knows what is most pleasurable to you. It speaks to the spiritual part of you that has its own preferences about living a life filled with pleasure. It is from this space that the Spiritual Hedonista routes for your joy and path to the most pleasurable life possible, created by following your own inner guidance.

Chapter 1: Be Your Own Guru

When you follow your own Inner Guidance, you are in touch with the power and the Creative Energy that created You and creates All That Is...

"Do I look fat?" This has to be one of the most frequently asked questions of another when trying on clothes and looking into the mirror. "Do I look fat in this? Does this look okay?" you ask your best friend or lover with the expectation of the reassurance that you look fabulous and are a divine Goddess (or God) no matter what is currently wrapped around your hips. "No, of course you don't look fat!" they exclaim back at you, "You look great." Not knowing whether or not you really believe them, you half-heartedly accept their reassurance and decide to wear that outfit, even though it feels 2 sizes too small and makes your gut look enormous. Why do we do this to ourselves? The Answer is simple: *we have not learned how to be our own gurus.* One may ask, "Well, how do I be my own guru when I can't even decide whether or not I look fat in my outfit?" Here's how....

How to be Your Own Guru:

1. Stop asking your friends, lovers and family whether or not you look fat in a particular outfit.
2. Get to know your gut (your instinctive, intuitive gut that is).
3. Sit in silence as often as you can everyday so that you get to know the sound of your own inner voice.
4. Know that your own inner voice is your guru.
5. Know that your gut is also your guru, otherwise known as instinct.
6. Stop listening to what other people are telling you.
7. Stop asking for other people's opinions.
8. Start asking yourself what your opinion is.
9. Start listening to your own opinions.

Most people spend more than half of their lives listening to the opinions of others and then taking action based upon those opinions. Don't you find that to be amazing? And less than half of their lives do they listen to themselves, their own opinions, their own instinct, and their own guidance based upon their feelings. Oftentimes, people who have made it a priority to cultivate their intuition and follow their gut instincts are seen as being selfish, because these people simply refuse to bow down to the opinions of others, making their own wishes and own desires their top priority. Where and when did we as a society come to the conclusion that this is a bad thing? Inner guidance is a spiritual gift and it is the most important tool one has to navigate through life. There is nothing more self-loving than to follow one's own feeling of comfort or discomfort. That feeling of comfort or discomfort in any situation is the communication of your own Inner Being, or Source Energy guiding you, letting you know if you are moving towards or away from that which you are wanting. Your positive feelings are guiding you towards what you want, and your negative feelings are a signal letting you know that you are currently in vibrational place that is leading you towards what you do not want. When you follow your own guidance you will ultimately benefit others through your alignment with your Source Energy. This is not inconsiderate of others' feelings. It is the ultimate act of consideration for your own feelings and it is in turn for others as well. And the reason why it is considerate for others is that by being true to yourself, you give others the freedom to choose whether or not they want to be involved with that which you truly are wanting. Be who you are and following your guidance, and allow *The Law of Attraction* to bring to you those others who are in alignment with Who You Really Are and that which you are wanting.

Be your own guru because, after many failed attempts at trying to be happy by listening to those outside of you, you will gradually over time realize that you are the only one who can hook onto that personal guidance system that you are born with. Only you know what you are feeling in any moment in time. Only you know which direction you are going in because only you can feel what your guidance is telling you. Being your own guru means following your own Inner Voice, intuition, gut instinct, whatever you want to call it. It is your own personal guidance system that only you and Source Energy know anything about. Cultivate the practice of being your own guru each and every day, and then each and every moment, and you will be guided towards all that you are desiring, and all that you are dreaming about.

Avid Daydreaming

Daydreaming is a form of visualizing, or creative visualization, in which one pleasurably envisions the life situation, object, or circumstances they wish to experience. This is a wonderful activity to engage in as often as you can on any given day, and it is an activity which can go for as long as your time or schedule allows. However, it is recommended that it be undertaken only for as long as it is pleasurable. It is the vibration of pleasure that is the most important element of this activity. The whole point of the activity is to feel good, to feel pleasure, and therefore increase your attraction of pleasurable experiences in your life. Most importantly, the point is to be, do, and have all that you are day dreaming or visualizing about in that moment-viscerally, through your cultivated feelings and focus on things that make you feel good. Even though a manifestation of what you want may have not yet occurred, you can still experience that which you desire through the power of your creative mind. The Universe acknowledges that what you are visualizing or daydreaming is already manifested in vibrational reality. What is necessary for the physical manifestation to occur is for you to line up vibrationally with what you have created in your mind. Abraham says that when one is in a vibrational place of feeling good, they are in a place to receive all that they are wanting. When one is in a vibrational place that is negative in feeling, they are emanating a vibration that will soon after attract that which is not wanted. When one continuously visualizes that which is unwanted, meaning, using the power of daydreaming to visualize things that one does not want, it is very likely that not long after a negative manifestation will occur.

This statement may cause one to ask, "Well, I'm sure that people don't visualize cancer, so how and why do they get that?" The answer to that is this: you attract through your vibration. While many images created by one's mind in a daydream or visualization manifest at a great speed for some, vibrations such as the vibration of cancer manifest over time by undetected or unmonitored negative thoughts which are allowed to exist and accumulate little by little over time. A person could have never day dreamed or visualized cancer. But they may have unknowingly had negative visualizations of worrisome, anger-inducing circumstances which induce a feeling of powerlessness. And by repeating these types of thoughts throughout the day, day after day, year after year, suddenly cancer appears. However, the manifestation was actually not sudden. It was a long accumulated habit of negative thoughts which one adjusted to over time. Basically, as with many people, the person who manifests cancer just gets used to not feeling good on one or many aspects in their life experience. These statements are not made to scare you. Millions of people vibrate themselves out of negative situations in all areas of life, including cancer and what you would consider to be worse things. Those who have practiced the *Law of Attraction* over time have vibrated themselves out of poverty, illness, abusive relationships, self-abuse, negativity, addictions, and virtually any type of negative thinking or destructive behaviour. It is focus on positive thoughts, focus on positive images, focus on moving toward the best feeling thought that you can find that brings you into a new vibrational frequency, and then eventually into new life circumstances.

Now the next question that may arise is, "Well, I really am not able to be positive. I'm really pissed off at that jerk that mistreated me and lied to me. How can I think a positive thought when I am in such a place of great anger?" And the answer to that is this: you do not have to be happy, rosy and smiley after someone lies to you, abuses you, or mistreats you. In fact, it is wonderful that you are not. Why? Because when you to stand right where you are, acknowledging yourself with clarity and understanding about where you are and how you feel, you are doing yourself a great service because now you are in a place to pivot your thoughts in the direction of what you are wanting. Once you know where you are, you can then make an effort to focus into a slightly better feeling and do the work of consciously and deliberately moving up what Abraham calls, the *Emotional Scale* (the scale of emotions ranging from joy and bliss on the high end, and powerlessness on the low end). So if you are really angry, do your best to think a less angry thought. Or, just express all of the anger you can in the safest way possible (in that you are not hurting yourself or others) and let yourself feel the relief of that. Relief is the order of the day. Relief is what you are reaching for. It is wonderful to be able to acknowledge your anger and then look towards the next best feeling thought, moving in that direction. Usually in the case of anger, the next best feeling thought would either be less anger or frustration. As you consciously talk yourself in the direction of better feeling thoughts, you get closer to that which you are wanting.

When you practice doing this, you begin to build your spiritual muscles and know your true power in creation. For when you understand and practice your power to vibrate yourself into greater connection with Your Source who is pure positive energy, you will then know your ability to create. Just the simple step from great anger to less anger is a demonstration of your True Power. And that is ENOUGH. You don't have to do any more than that right now. There is a stream of well-being that will naturally carry you towards better feeling thoughts. All you need is the desire to move there rather than holding onto the banks of the current, meaning holding on to those negative thoughts that keep you away from what you want.

It is best that you do only what brings relief to you with the least amount of effort, and in a way that feels natural for you. Oftentimes what happens is that you get distracted from the subject that is bringing you negative emotion, drop the subject for a while, and upon revisiting the subject you feel better than you did before without having to do anything about it. And better does not necessarily mean happy, but better may be that yesterday you were really angry, and today you feel frustrated, which is a better feeling than being really angry. As you trust the natural process and deliberately reach for a better feeling thought, you'll soon find that you move from frustration, to less frustration, to a little bit of pessimism, then into contentment, and eventually into hope. And once you are hopeful, hopeful for better circumstances, hopeful in understanding the lesson in your recent experience, hopeful that a better person for you is just around the corner, then you got it, because just around the corner from hope is belief, then knowing and, once you KNOW, and stay in that vibration, a new manifestation occurs. See how it works?

Avid Meditating

Just as with day dreaming, meditation is another wonderful way to feel better and to raise your vibration to a better feeling place. Meditation is the act of releasing thought and quieting the mind. Oftentimes meditations start out or end up being a session of daydreaming, but after some practice a true quieting of the mind will gradually take place. During the meditation period one connects to their non-physical energy which is the connection to all that is. One of the greatest values in daily meditation is that one becomes familiar with this connection and acknowledgement of the non-physical energy which flows through them and is able to carry it with them and breathe that energy into their daily activities. The reason why people admire the great athletes, artists, entrepreneurs, and the many other people who are at the top of their fields, is because they are experts at connecting to their non-physical energy and letting it shower all over their activities. Many of these people do not even realize that this is what is happening and describe it as, "just doing what I feel passionate about," or, "being really stubborn and insisting on doing what I want." Both of these statements are reflections of their alignment with Source Energy, regardless of their belief or disbelief in non-physical energy. These people whom we admire have cultivated the act of being their own gurus and following their inner guidance, acting from inspiration, rather than from motivation. Their actions are inspired from their communication with Source Energy, in their understanding of what feels good. They are experts at moving in the direction of what feels good. Oftentimes, they simple ask themselves, "Which choice feels better?" They are well practiced at taking the better feeling choices- that's it!

Practice Makes Perfect

Being your own guru is a lot easier said than done. However, as with any new skill, *practice does make perfect*. It takes a while to change long-practiced habits, particularly in a society which predominantly supports a paradigm where there are experts that the masses need to follow (since these apparent experts apparently know more about You than You do). One might even argue that this book is in and of itself is a form of an expert giving advice from a place of, "Follow me, I know what I am doing more than you do." But really this book is one human being sharing with another human being what has worked successfully, without guarantees that it is a cure-all, but with an assurance that it is a formula that has worked very well and has been passed down from the masters to those who will listen and who have faith in following through with something that requires self-love and focus. It is a guide offered in a Spirit of Love, to help you find the freedom from the self-imposed boundaries created over time which are keeping you from all that you are wanting: the relationships, the money, the bodily conditions, and the happiness and peace of mind you long for on a regular basis. But in order to follow this guide, you have to be able to cultivate a relationship with your own Inner Guidance, and release yourself from the opinions of others.

Freedom from the Opinions of Others

There is such a tremendous freedom that you will gain once you learn to regularly release yourself from the opinions of others. People's opinions are coming from their own selfish perspective of what they want from you and how *they* believe you should be living your life. They may even be coming from a place of love, but Love does not care what decisions you make or do not make. Love cares about how you are feeling in response to the decisions you are making. In other words, if you make a decision that makes you feel bad, Love gives you an indicator of a negative emotion or a feeling of discomfort, which indicates that the decision you are making is leading you towards an unwanted outcome. Love also gives you an indicator of positive emotion when you make a decision that is about to bring you a positive, or wanted outcome. Most of the time, the decision does not really matter. What does matter is how you feel in response to the decision and how you feel in response to yourself and your own life experience in relation to the decision. Other people's decisions are irrelevant to you, because only you know how you feel and what is in your heart. Only you know how you are feeling in response to what is going on around you. Learning how to let go of the opinions of others is not always easy, and it is especially important during this process to be extra kind to yourself every step of the way.

Be Kind to Yourself Every Step of the Way

It is so important to be kind to yourself every step of the way during your process of changing your thoughts. It is not easy to change lifelong ways of thinking and being. If you would have known about this stuff before it is highly likely that you would have made choices which were more in the direction of what you truly desire. No need to worry. A large majority of the world's population follows the crowd and has very little concept of following's one's internal guidance. Humans are for the most part not socialized to do so. So please be kind to yourself. The moment you start beating up on yourself or feeling discouragement you are going against yourself and going against the direction of what you truly want. Being critical or unkind to yourself for not being where you want to be is counteractive to your growth and well-being. Love yourself and stay on your path. If you continuously soothe yourself and love yourself as best you can all along the way, not only will your journey be joyful, you will head straight towards what you are wanting and will be able to look back on your journey with a feeling of pleasure and joy. Wherever you start your journey is okay. Respect your feelings all along the way in the Spirit of self-love that you deserve.

Respect Your Own Feelings

It is utterly imperative that you respect your own feelings and know what they are! So many people walk around this beautiful planet, not knowing who they are, not knowing how they feel, and repeating the sentiments of others as if they were their own. They have programmed themselves so well, for so long, for years in fact, to listen to what others are saying, take the opinions of those others to heart, and live by their standards. What kind of life is that? There is no joy in that. Joy cannot exist when one is disconnected from his or herself. Joy does not reside in that type of environment. Joy can only be accessed by one who has self-love, self-respect, and self-kindness. That is the only way in which joy will eventually appear on and be a part of one's path. By respecting your own feelings, you are acknowledging that you are an ever evolving being who came here to create, and any negative emotion that you feel is guidance. This guidance is important and valuable- not something that should give you a reason to beat up on yourself. Negative emotion is guidance. Positive emotion is guidance as well. Your feelings are you guidance system, and your guidance system is helping you to get to where you want to be. In respecting your feelings, you will better understand where you are in relation to where you want to be, and you will also better understand what your resistance points are.

Resistance Points

According to Abraham we all have resistance points on various subjects in our lives. These are points of resistance where we have not allowed our natural well-being to flow; hence, they are points where one has resisted the flow of goodness into their lives. Have you ever known anyone who is completely in their power when it comes to money and finances but are horrible in relationships? Or have you known the opposite: someone who is wonderful when it comes to relationships but cannot balance a check book? We all have places in our lives where we are in touch with our power and places where we are not. Sometimes we are in touch with our power when it comes to our relationships with our pets, handling a difficult boss, painting, baking, cooking, cleaning, or any other matter of subjects in which we engage in during day-to-day life. As each subject comes up throughout the day, it is good to begin to take notice of the feelings that you have surrounding that subject. Sometimes your feelings feel high-flying and positive, while on other subjects your feelings may feel negative or hopeless. It does not matter where you stand on each subject because only you can emit your own vibration, and other people's experiences are irrelevant to your own personal experience.

Even if you are living under the same roof, it is completely possible to live a completely different life from those who are in your immediate surroundings. You need not live a life experience where you are looking around at 'what is' or repeating 'what is'. This is the habit of most humans on the planet. When you practice focusing in the direction of what it is that you are truly wanting, you begin to attract, people, circumstances and events that are more and more a reflection of what you are wanting to experience in life. The process is oftentimes gradual. But once you are aware of the way you feel on various subjects, then it is easier to be able to focus in the direction of what you are wanting even if you are standing in a very negative place. Everyone starts somewhere, and it does not matter where you start, it matters that you stick with it. And the reason why it is important to stick with it is because your success is inevitable. Your attainment of what you desire is guaranteed if you keep walking in the direction of it. So no matter where or what your resistance point is, it can always be changed.

You could currently be standing in a place of feeling very worried about money, which is what your resistance point is-'worry'. If you continue to sooth your worry, having conversations with yourself as you would with someone you love and care about, and sooth yourself into better feeling thoughts, you will be walking in the direction of plenty of money even though you may currently be in a place that is far from it. If you keep walking in that direction, eventually you will get there. It would be foolish to turn around and go back just because you temporarily do not see the physical manifestation of the money. Abraham oftentimes uses the example of travelling from Phoenix to San Diego when describing one's journey between where they are and where they want to be. In this example, it would be foolish to turn around and go back to Phoenix, just because you have not yet seen the signs which say, "Welcome to San Diego". If you keep a steady pace, you will eventually get to San Diego. This analogy can be used for all journeys towards things which one is looking to manifest. As long as you stay moving in the direction of that which you want, meaning, feeling better and better about the subject, you will eventually get there. It is the feeling journey that Abraham emphasizes, not the action journey. When you focus on improving your feelings, the actions will be inspired. Acting from inspiration is the feeling of not being able to avoid the action because you feel so inspired to take it. There is no hesitation involved because the action is coming from a place of alignment with Source, and it just feels like the next logical step. In your path towards joy about any subject, you are getting closer to what you want. Your joy is the indicator that you are on the brink of a desired manifestation. This is why it is important to cultivate as much joy in your life as possible.

Being Trained Out of Your Joy

Society does a heck of a job training you out of your joy. From morning, noon, to night the media blasts into your television, and now your laptops and mobile phones, the horrors of this world as if that is all that there is. And by the *Law of Attraction*, meaning that which is like unto itself is drawn, if you train yourself to those frequencies you too could be one of those horrible stories that you see daily on the news. This statement is not meant to scare you: it is to make you aware of how much negative vibration you intake each and every day. You must learn to love yourself enough to monitor the sources of media you intake. You must love yourself enough to turn off the television and pay attention to what you are feeling and the inner guidance that is being offered to you- that is something that you definitely cannot find through the internet or a television set.

While not all media is negative in nature, a large amount of it is. So quite simply, out of self-love, you must be aware of what you are taking in, and focus upon media that makes you feel good, so that you do not allow outside influences to train you out of your natural state of joy. It is true that Source Energy can speak to you through the internet, television, a song, or other means of communication. Have you ever had one of those experiences where you watched a commercial that touched your heart and reminded you to call someone that you have been thinking about for a long time? Even better still, using the same example, has it ever happened to you that a specific person you were reminded of when watching that commercial, emails you out of the blue? These are not happenstance coincidences- these are evidences of Source Energy connecting with you and communicating to you in a language in which you can understand, a language which can only get in through your crack of least resistance.

What is a Crack of Least Resistance?

Source Energy knows that you will only pay attention to It according to your current belief set points. If you currently do not believe that Source Energy can communicate with you through channelling (such as what Esther Hicks does with Abraham), then Source Energy will not try to communicate with you in that fashion. But if you believe that Source Energy can send you a sign, like through a commercial, through a song, through an email, or through a phone call, then Source Energy will do that. Source Energy wants to communicate with you and have you receive the message, because that is what your inner being is wanting. You are connected to all that Is. Your crack of least resistance is that small space where you will allow something in. It is that small space of possibly an email, or a phone call, or a commercial that you allow in without resistance, in which Source Energy can enter because It knows that you will let that in anyway. That is your crack of least resistance. You see, abundance, and all that Source Energy is, is available to you at all times, but most people do not allow all of it in due to their practiced belief systems. This is why it is important to feel good as much as possible in order for that crack of least resistance to get bigger.

One will notice that through practiced meditation over time their crack gets bigger, for practicing meditation often results in becoming more comfortable and familiar with silence. This is when true acknowledgement of connection takes place. You are always connected to Source Energy at all times, but oftentimes, in fact, most of the time human beings cut themselves off through paying attention to things that bother them. When you focus upon what you are wanting, rather than the things that bother you, you open yourself up to Source Energy and becoming a vibrational match to all of the things that you are wanting. In essence, through your focus upon the things that you want, you open up your crack of least resistance so that all that you desire can flood into your life.

Focus on What You Want, and
Ignore What You Don't Want

Repeating to yourself, "Focus on what you want, and ignore what you don't want," will help you to practice doing so on a regular basis. The more you repeat an idea, the more it will make sense to you, and the more it makes sense to you, the easier it is to believe. Pay attention to the things that you want. And if the things that you want are nowhere around you, go there in your mind. And if you cannot go there in your mind, find one thing, one easily accessible thing, such as the beauty of the changing leaves in a park, to focus upon. These moments of beauty will help bring you back to your connection with Who You Really Are and Who You Are Meant to Be. It is magical what can happen over time of repeated focusing either in your mind through imagination or during your present waking hours of focusing on the beauty of an autumn leaf or the gorgeousness of the blending of colours in a sunset. Focusing on the rhythms and harmonies of a beautiful piece of music and the laughter of children playing in a playground are such marvellous ways to experience an increased connection to that part of you which is pure Love and pure Joy. And the more you focus upon things that thrill you or make your heart sing, the more things that you are wanting will come into your experience. And they come into your experience, because through your practiced feel-good vibration, you have become a vibrational match to all the things that you want.

There are feel-good pleasures which are available to all at no cost, and focusing upon them will raise your vibration. The Universe does not deprive you. Yes-you may as a Spiritual being have chosen to be born into early circumstances of poverty or deprivation. However, you knew darn well as a Spiritual being that you could vibrate out of those circumstances. Those horrific contrasting experiences would cause you to want for yourself and others in such an enormous way that the circumstance of being born into a feathered nest would not extract from you. You knew as a Spiritual being that being born into a feathered nest would not serve your purpose of being a great creator. You said, "Alright-bring on the contrast. Because I know that vibrating out of it will be so delicious and exhilarating, and with that valuable comparison between what is wanted and what is not, I will be able to experience Who I Really Am in the deepest of ways. Go on. Bring it on. I have no fear, for I know that You are with me wherever I go."

Divine Guidance is With You Wherever You Go

Being your own guru means knowing that Divine Guidance is with you wherever you go, so you don't have to listen to other people. Most people have forgotten who they really are and are not connected to their own Divine Guidance. And those disconnected ones have nothing to offer to you anyway, because all things of true help and value come from a place of connection with Source. Anything less than that is a diminishment of who you really are and what you have to offer. Connect to your own Divine Guidance and all of your questions will be answered in a way that you can hear it. Connect with your Divine Guidance and experience what it is truly like to be your own guru. For that Divine Guidance is your highest self, your inner being, which is connected to all things, people and circumstances that no mere human eye can see. It knows you. It recognizes you. It acknowledges you. It appreciates you. And most of all, it knows your true genius potential as a Divine Creator, even if your human mind does not.

Getting Into the Vortex and Letting Your Trail Light Up For You

Abraham so lovingly and wonderfully coined the term, *The Vortex*, which is a vibrational place where all of your dreams and desires reside. By getting into the

Vortex, a place in your mind, but more importantly, in your 'feeling' (solar plexus, gut) where your ideal life exists, you are connecting to the Energy and Power that creates worlds. Believe it or not, the Vortex is not this far, far away place that can only be accessed in a dream state. It is a vibrational place which is accessible in the here and now- you just have to practice going there as often as possible in order to become a vibrational match to It.

It may be helpful to try and recall your feelings as a child when you would play your most favourite games, or the feelings that you had as a teenager in love for the first time and being told that you were loved back. These are just some small examples of what the Vortex feels like: this swirling, magnificent place where there is no such thing as doubt and where things just manifest because you know that they will and because your anticipation of them is so strong that the Universe can't help but give it to you. The Vortex feels like magic because it is, and because *You Are Magic*. This everyday magic is what is truly normal for a powerful, deliberate creator. Getting everything that you want is normal for the one who knows their Vortex and to whom their Vortex has become their best friend. Get into the Vortex as often as possible throughout the day, and your trail will light up for you. The next logical steps to take will be so clear for you, for clarity only shows up when you are in the Vortex.

Feel as good as you possibly can and find any way that you can to do it, and you will be in your Vortex where the answers are, where your clarity is, and where your path to all that you want lights up.

Remember Your Successes

One sure way of getting into the Vortex is to remember your successes, big and little. Remember the times in your life where you felt powerful, gorgeous, special, and completely and totally loved. Replay them in your mind. And while you replay those scenarios in your mind, say to yourself, "See, I created that. I can do this. I have done this before. I didn't even realize I was doing it a lot of the time. I am experienced at this and now that I am aware of the Laws of the Universe, I can create experiences like this again and again, and again! I am so excited about what is to come and where I am going. I am so excited to apply this feeling to my next creation." Remember your successes, and practice that high flying feeling that you get when you remember them. For this high flying feeling is what your Vortex is all about. And when that feeling becomes so familiar to you, and you practice it again and again, it will soon become your normal set-point of attraction. And a set-point of attraction which is of bliss, joy, appreciation, and love, is the vibrational vantage point which will attract all the things that you are wanting: the lover, the money, the well-being, the health, the vitality, the joy, and the bliss that you are looking for. You came to this physical life experience to live all of that, and most importantly, to create it. Life can be so sweet when you get into the Vortex and revel over your successes.

Chapter 2: A Spoonful or More of Sugar Everyday

Life is Sweet when you make it a priority to make it Sweet-each and Every Day...

Life could be so much sweeter than it is today, and it can be even sweeter than it is tomorrow. These are difficult words to hear if you are in the midst of an unwanted experience or dealing with a problem. However, remind yourself that all of this life experience is temporary, and that what you are experiencing today need not be repeated tomorrow. You have creative control of your life experience through the control of your vibration. And while you cannot control other people, you can control your vibration by choosing the thoughts that you think. The more you practice better feeling thoughts and thoughts of self-love and respect, the higher your frequency will raise, and you will open the floodgates to that which you want. In times of trouble, do your best to focus upon yourself and how you feel. With practice, you can focus yourself into better feeling thoughts, and shortly thereafter, better feeling circumstances. Life is supposed to be sweet, simple and fun. Really, it is!

Believe it or not, the purpose of your life is joy. You have not come to this earth to accumulate as many accomplishments as possible, although you are free to do so. Most people around the world have been socialized to believe in many different things about this life experience, and predominantly, those things are associated and related to suffering and working hard. "There's no gain without pain," is a popular and often repeated mantra by the masses. There is no karmic retribution or punishment in this life. This life is truly, purely, about being in joy and experiencing joy through your growth and expansion. Yes, there are things that exist that you do not want, which Abraham refers to as 'contrast'. But a continued practice of focusing on what you do want, thinking thoughts that feel good and are loving towards yourself and others, and experiencing as much pleasure as possible, will raise your vibration swiftly and easily. You will create a sweet life by doing this. This is the basis of what Spiritual Hedonism is all about.

Spiritual Hedonism is about experiencing the sweetness of life through every one of your six senses: your hearing, smelling, tasting, touching, seeing, and intuiting. Life can be experienced with such sweetness, that it is possible for a human being to live a majority of his or her life in ecstasy and joy despite all that goes on around them. Even if what goes on around them is negative in nature, it is possible to experience the pure joy of one's inner being and live and choose the path of pleasure so consistently to the point that one vibrates out of negative circumstances and situations. Your consistent acknowledgement of the divine energy within you that is free from the perceived bad behaviour of others will help you to vibrate out of circumstances which you deem to be unwanted. Out of a desire to experience the sweetness of life and to experience love to the fullest you can train your thoughts in a direction which will create a life of fun and joy for you. You can vibrate yourself out of anything (if that is what you want)!

What do you mean by vibrating your way out of things?

Esther and Jerry Hicks through their translations of the non-physical entity called, *Abraham*, are the master teachers of the concept of vibration. They teach that the *Law of Attraction* applies to every being's life experience- no exception. We are all vibrational beings first, before we are flesh, blood and bone beings. The vibrations that we emanate determine our point of attraction. Our feelings are the indicators of how we are vibrating. We attract according to the way we feel. So for example, if you are feeling beautiful, you will attract experiences that reflect that.

The manifestations you may experience are people consistently complimenting you on your beauty or choices of attire. You may manifest experiences of the admiration of many. Have you ever seen someone like this? The best example can be found by looking into society and observing the people who are considered to be beautiful by the masses. You may very well find that some of those people are not beautiful by your own personal standards. But because *they* believe that they are beautiful, they emanate that vibration and in turn attract the experiences of adoration for their perceived beauty. It truly is about the *Law of Attraction.* And the reason why this is so is because Source Energy only creates that which is beautiful- we just choose as individuals to believe in the beauty we possess or not.

If you want to vibrate out of a situation into a new one, you simply have to focus the majority of your attention upon what you are wanting. Through visualizing, daydreaming, or through activities which release resistance like meditation or taking a nap, you will be able to gradually shift your vibration into that which you are wanting. The most important thing is to feel as good as you can on any given subject. When you are feeling good, you are in the vicinity of drawing the manifestation to you. But this feeling good part needs to be fairly consistent, and people feel differently about different subjects. It is good to start off feeling as best as you can first on any given subject, even if feeling best is feeling angry (which is totally fine). Allow yourself to slowly and gradually move up the emotional scale as Abraham calls it, from right where you are. The Universe is there to assist you. You are never alone in this process. And this process is to be done in a kind and loving way towards yourself. There is no right or wrong. There is just the relativity of feeling worse, or feeling better- that's it. The Universe understands what you have gone through that has prompted you to feel the way that you feel. The Universe has seen all that has happened which may have incited anger within you. There is no judgement in this. There is only Source Energy routing for you to feel better, and calling you towards that better feeling place.

New Manifestations are a Reflection of a New Vibration

Have you ever gone back to the home where you grew up and noticed that nothing has changed? Or maybe you are currently at the home where you grew up and feel frustration at the fact that nothing has changed? Do you know how this happens? When a human being offers a vibration, manifestation soon after occurs. If a human keeps on offering the same vibration, then the same or similar manifestation occurs. A person can live his or her lifetime re-creating same circumstances and experiences in this way. Time may have passed, but because they keep offering the same vibrations, the same or similar manifestations occur. These seemingly 'same' manifestations are really new manifestations, but they are a replica of the old manifestations because they were created from the same vibration. The faces may have changed, the names may have changed, but the circumstances feel the same. The key to change is to offer a *new* vibration. This can be a process which feels unfamiliar and potentially uncomfortable initially, because it is new and different from what has been offered over a long period of time for many. That is okay, because change usually feels a bit strange at first.

You know that you have changed your vibration when the manifestations around you have changed. And you know that you have changed your vibration into something more wanted when you are experiencing more and more of what is wanted to you personally, keeping other people's wants or opinions completely out of the equation. This change usually happens gradually, and gradual change is very effective. When small changes occur, it is almost like you are little by little giving yourself the evidence which you are seeking that says, "Hey, this stuff really does work." When you witness the small evidence that changing your thoughts will bring to you, the process becomes easier to believe. Most people have been trained to believe that believing is seeing and not the other way around, so they do not believe that change or good things are possible until they see them first. However, this is a catch 22, because change cannot come unless one believes it first- then eventually the manifestations of the change will be visible.

Some manifestations occur almost instantly. For instance, when you have a thought such as, "I ran out of milk. I need to go to the store to buy milk." You don't doubt that the milk will be available at the store. For the most part, you don't doubt your ability to pay for the milk. You don't say, "I don't know. Buying more milk seems impossible. I don't know if I can do it. I don't know if it will be available, I don't know if I can afford it, I don't know if I can trust the storekeeper to stock his supply with milk..." It seems absurd to go through this line of thinking in regards to a simple purchase of milk when one runs out of it. But this is exactly what most humans do all of the time when considering the manifestation of what they want- they doubt, they over-analyze, they question, they doubt their ability, they doubt other's ability, they doubt the Universe in its ability to supply. This happens so often, that they either don't try, or they do try, but then turn around and go back home because they feel that their efforts to go to the store to buy milk are silly and that they are being a 'dreamer'. It is the natural way of the Universe to supply you with that which you want.

Abraham's words, "Ask and it is Given," best describe the process of creating between you and the Universe. When you ask for something, whether it is through your words or through your thoughts, the Universe answers it right away. When you run out of milk and you ask for more- it is given. You just have to know that it is there for you and expect to get it. If you don't expect the milk, then you won't get the milk. It is really that simple. Offer a vibration of expectancy, no matter how big or small the desire is, and you will get it. "It is just as easy to create a castle as it is a button," Abraham says, "but most of you have buttons because they are easier to expect." The Universe will give you what you expect regardless of its size or perceived difficulty. The issue is practicing the vibration of expectancy and staying on that vibrational frequency. It's pretty easy to do with a carton of milk. Now your work is to apply that same expectancy to other wanted things or circumstances in your life. You deserve it- that is a given. You have the ability to create it- that is also a given. Now you are cultivating the knowledge of how to do so. Practice makes perfect. But it is always fun and easy to start raising your vibration by focusing on things that you love.

What Do You Love? What Would Make Your Life A Little Bit Sweeter Today?

Do you love to start your day with a sweet hot cup of tea or coffee? Do you love a morning pastry or a beautiful glass of wine with dinner? These delicious and sweet treats are such a wonderful way of celebrating your life today. They may seem small, but they certainly go a long way in terms of shifting your mood into a more positive direction. This is not advice to ingest food or drink that you don't want, nor an encouragement to consume any substance as a substitute for your alignment with Source. However, it is a suggestion that little treats for your Self, whether they be edible or inedible, are a way of expressing gratitude for the wonderful and simple things in life that are there for your enjoyment. These are things which you can easily afford or create which will bring a smile to your face and remind you of life's goodness. Whether that treat comes in the form of a sweet cup of coffee, a walk in the park during your lunch break, or a stroll along the river at night, these treats are really a great way to show yourself how you love yourself and how you are willing to do fun and sweet things for yourself to make your day ever the more brighter. These are simple suggestions of ways that you can feel pleasure everyday on your own, without having to involve other people. They are pleasures which you can enjoy during quiet intimate times between you and your Source

Energy. It is the way of a spiritual hedonist to enjoy the pleasures of life, big or small, in simple and sweet ways, between themselves and Source Energy.

Hang Around People Who Are Supportive of Your Dreams, and If There is No One Like That, Hang Out With Yourself

It is so important to be mindful of the company you keep. It is so important not to squander your precious energy discussing with people your dreams if you know that they will either mock you, disagree with you, or discourage you from what is so true to you and pulsing within the deepest depths of your being. It is always best to keep your precious dreams to yourself. When you do this, you keep your dreams between You and your Source Energy, who are the only key components to manifesting your desires anyway. Source will attract all that you need including the right people who are necessary to help make your dreams a reality. A disconnected human cannot help you in any way. And even if they are connected, it is not their job to make your dreams come true. Your dreams are between you and Source Energy. If you believe that you need another's approval or validation then you are not in the vibrational realm of receiving your dreams- for in your connection with Source, no approval or validation is required.

You will know that you are truly connected to Source when you can dream, and dream, and dream, and not feel the need to tell another. When you are connected there is an absolute knowing of your worthiness to receive and a trust that the Universe is there to provide for you. True connection means a releasing of all doubt, worry, fear, anxiety, feelings of inadequacy, and concern for the opinions of others. For in your knowing and expectation, you will be able to watch the Universal forces knock Itself out to make your dreams a reality. That is when you know you are connected. If you are not there or nowhere near there- no worries. Just facing in that direction will get you there- no action or effort is required. As Abraham says, there is a stream of abundance of all good things which flows for all. All you need to do is to let go of your oars of resistance to the stream and flow downstream in the direction of it. Manifestation is supposed to feel effortless, joyful, and fun.

Effortless Manifestation

Have you ever been prompted by another to recall a name of a specific person and have completely forgotten it, even though the name is on the tip of your tongue? But then several hours later you recall it randomly with no effort? Well that scenario is a prime example of what effortless manifestation is all about:

letting the Universe know that there is something that you really want, letting go of the desire and releasing it to the Universe, and then allowing it to come to you without you having to do anything about it.

All creation that is in alignment with Who You Really Are, Source Energy, is effortless. Go back again to your past successes. Can you pick out ones that came to you unexpectedly? Are you finding that most came to you seemingly out of the blue? Are you finding that most if not all of them just worked out for you effortlessly, while you were feeling great, and people called you, 'lucky'? These are not examples of luck: they are examples of times in your life when you were successful at raising your vibration to one that was composed of a high flying, excited about life feeling, where you knew your power to create and trusted completely in your gifts and talents. These were times when you knew that you are a special and unique individual who has special and unique gifts to offer to the world in a way that no one else in the world can offer them. These were the times when you were so in touch with Source that the Universe bent over backwards to accommodate your feeling because your vibration was so strong and powerful it could not help but grant you your wishes. This is what effortless manifestation is all about. Find ways to be thrilled with where you stand right now, and focus on your future becoming with such fearless anticipation that the Universal forces just find the most intricate and detailed ways to rush those manifestations into your experience. This is all the work of the mind. There is no physical effort involved. There is such a huge disparity between the actual physical effort exerted between 'logically doing the right thing' and acting because you absolutely can't help but act (meaning acting from inspiration). Abraham refers to this as, *inspired action.*

If someone called you up, a legitimate person whom you trusted, and said, "Meet me at 3pm today: you have just inherited 1 million dollars and it will be delivered to you at my office during the reading of a will." Would you hesitate to go? Would you complain about having to get dressed and bring your physical body over there in whatever mode of transportation would be suitable for that time being? Most would believe it to be absurd to label those actions as effortful. For while physical actions are taking place (for example, you may have to take a shower, go to your closet and pick out something to wear, refill your travel card, or fill up your gas tank,) these actions are in no way effortful because they are a part of bringing you towards an action that is so in alignment with your dreams, that you may not even notice that you are doing them because you are so filled with excited anticipation, that the shower will feel great to you! The filling up of your travel card will feel wonderful to you because you know that you may never have to take public transportation again unless you really want to! All of these actions feel effortless, because they are inspired actions. All inspired action feels effortless.

Now for a few seconds, it is of value to look at the flip side. How does it feel to get up and take a shower to go to a job that you hate? How does it feel to fill up your metro card before you have to head to the office working for a boss that you loathe? All of these actions feel effortful and dreadful. However, if this example speaks to your current situation there is nothing to fear. For through the power of your mind you can coach yourself into a positive thought arena about all of the things that are bothering you. And once you train yourself into this more positive arena, your vibration will move to a higher frequency, and you will gradually vibrate yourself out of these current uncomfortable and unwanted situations. All that it takes is a moment to moment awareness of how you feel. And once you know how you feel in response to a specific topic, all you now have to do is to reach for a better feeling thought. You can do this simple work for each and every topic as it arises in your life. Through focusing on the things that are working for you, even if it is just one thing out of 25, focus on that one thing, bless that one thing, and you will move into a more positive direction. All situations, all current manifestations, and all current reality are just a temporary indication of a temporary vibration. As your thoughts shift, and your vibrations shift, your manifestations will reflect those changes. This is usually a gradual process. It is always helpful to start your path of effortless manifestation by doing things that bring you pleasure in order to increase the good-feeling vibrations within you.

The Pleasure Principle

The famous psychoanalyst, Sigmund Freud, created a theory called, *The Pleasure Principle*, which basically states that humans gravitate towards experiences of pleasure and avoid experiences of pain. On a spiritual level, it is good to note that many humans gravitate towards experiences of pain not because they want to, since most do so unknowingly out of habit. And these habits were created by following the misguided advice of disconnected others and practicing that advice over time. Regardless of where you are or where you have been, you can start bringing more pleasure into your life TODAY, which is the only day that matters. Today is the only day that you have to work with. You cannot work with tomorrow, because it has not come yet, and you cannot work with yesterday, because it is already gone. All you need to do is to work with your NOW. And in your *now*, you must move towards what is pleasurable in order to increase your happiness. You must make frequent and regular pleasure a priority in order to live a full and joyful life experience on this physical planet. To move towards pain is meaningless and just produces more pain. Moving towards pleasure produces more pleasure. And given a choice, would you choose a pleasureable life or a painful life? The answer may seem obvious, but start to observe how often you move towards pleasure and how often you move towards pain. And when you notice yourself moving towards pain, just stop doing that and shift your attention elsewhere. It may seem simplistic, but the simple act of doing this will gradually and eventually make the feeling of pain so foreign to you, that you are no longer willing to tolerate it. Therefore, you will truly be practicing the *Pleasure Principle* to the benefit of your happiness, joy, pleasure, and well-being.

It is important to note that this suggestion does not mean to do or consume things that bring pleasure in the moment but then bring pain to you shortly thereafter, such as binge eating, taking narcotics, or engaging in sexual activity that you will regret later, which will eventually lead to a crash, or a painful experience. While Source Energy never judges you on the ways that you choose to feel better, it knows that you can conjure up ways to feel pleasure without having to experience any kind of unwanted experience in association with the pleasurable experience. It is also good to note that this type of crash or roller coaster behaviour usually stems from an underlying belief that one should be punished for engaging in pleasure out of a feeling of not being deserving of it. Source Energy wants you to experience a life of pleasure in an uninhibited, worthy, stress-free way, free from crashes, regret, drama, or pain. It is possible. And not only is it possible, it is the natural way for a Source Energy being to experience life. There are many choices to make when it comes to experiencing pleasure in life, not just a few. And there are many pleasurable experiences to enjoy in this life which have no negative or unwanted after effects. Beauty and pleasure are all around you if you line yourself up with Source Energy.

Most humans have come to believe that there are things in life that they have to put up with and that pain is an inevitable part of the human experience. Source does not deny that pain exists and that pain can occur in one's life experience. However, pain is seen to be one of the possibilities available as a part of a contrasting life experience. It can be seen as a choice. You don't have to recreate pain over and over again until you are numb and consider pain to be normal. Because pain is not normal. Nor does it serve you to believe that pain is normal. Joy is normal. Pleasure is normal. Most humans just don't believe that so they continue to create drama after painful drama, never moving towards all the things that they want and deserve. Focus on what pleases you. Focus on the things that you find pleasure in doing, whether it be baking a cake, singing, painting, watching the sunset, writing poetry, reading your child a bed time story, or any number of the variety of things and activities available to you. It is the focus on, "How can I bring more pleasure to my life today?" that will attract more pleasurable experiences into your life on an everyday basis.

So, the Spiritual Hedonista's *Pleasure Principle* would be: move towards pleasure and move towards only pleasure. The more pleasure you seek, the more pleasure you will experience. And then soon enough, a pleasurable life will become the new normal for you.

Love Your Self Everyday!

Why don't the literary powers that be change the famous quote, "How do I love thee, let me count the ways?" to, "How do I Love Me, Let Me count the ways!" It's amazing how easy it is for most of us to love others first and foremost and completely forget about ourselves. There is such an imbalance in society in which humans believe that self-sacrifice and deprivation are wonderful and impressive qualities and that selfishness is abhorrent. Abraham teaches selfishness in that they (the collective consciousness that Abraham is) states, "If you are not selfish enough to align yourself with Source, you have nothing to offer anyone anyway." A softer, gentler way of saying this would be, "If you don't love yourself enough to align with Source, you will have nothing to offer anyone because all things of value come from alignment with Source."

When Abraham uses the word 'selfish', it does not imply that one should disregard other people's feelings in a spirit of lack of consideration. It simply means that if one is not selfish enough, or self-loving enough to value their own feelings, then they cannot offer anything to anyone else in a spirit of love. Most people disregard their own feelings and give to others in a spirit of obligation, 'saving face', or 'trying to keep the peace'. A true gift is one that is given in a spirit of love and alignment. It is best not to offer anything at all unless it comes from this space. One can be selfish, and generous, and considerate, all at the same time. If one is selfish enough to make lining up with Source their top priority, then generosity and consideration are a natural result of that alignment. If you give to yourself first and make sure that you are full, then everything else is just an overflow which is easily and can be joyously given to others from a place of true abundance.

There are various cultures around the planet which advocate gift-giving as a form of politeness and obligation. While this is all a part of the Universe's contrast and most definitely should be allowed, it is a custom which was not created from a place of alignment. Most people, if they were really to be honest with themselves, would not feel comfortable accepting a gift if they knew that the person giving it was just doing it out of obligation and really had no warm feelings whatsoever towards the recipient. Giving in this way is not healthy. It is a form of manipulation which is disconnected from Source Energy. Your connected to Source Energy Self is self-sufficient and does not need, obligate, or coerce. It gives from a place of pure abundance and joy, regardless of what is given in return or not.

If everyone acted from a place of alignment, everyone would get what they want without fearing that if someone else gets what they want that they will lose out. The Universe is abundant. Love yourself enough to remind yourself that the Universe is abundant and that the Universe will provide you with the things that are in harmony with what you want. There is no need for coercion when you are in alignment with the laws of the Universe. There is only self-sufficiency, independence, and healthy interaction with one another and most importantly, with one's Self. Love yourself each and every day, and you will gradually learn to make healthier, more loving choices for yourself which will ultimately benefit others in a powerful way. You teach through your example, and you can love through your example of alignment.

Chapter 3: Making Peace with the Hot, Spicy, Salty, & Sweet

The Universe is filled with such Delicious Diversity- you don't have to devour all of it, just choose and focus upon the things that you like and ignore the things that you don't like...

There is such a rich amount of diversity on this planet and in this life experience. If there was not a richness of diversity on this planet you could not be who you are, and you could not stand where you stand. And the reason for this is because you have become what you are today because of your focus and the choices you have made out of the variety available to you. This planet is one of relativity and contrast. You are where you are, and someone else is where they are, all as a result of individual focusing. Some of your creations are wanted and some of them are not wanted. Whatever has resulted from your choices and focus is okay. From the perspective of Source Energy, it is just variety. It is the human mind that prescribes meaning and definition to that which they choose.

Every moment is a chance to begin anew if one so desires, and choose the same or differently through focus. The diversity on this planet is the blessed contrast which Abraham speaks often about and is the bountiful set of ingredients which one can choose to focus upon. Contrast gives deliberate creators the chance to choose. It gives deliberate creators an opportunity to choose what to focus upon and therefore create.

If we lived on a homogenous planet where everyone looked the same, spoke the same, thought the same, and did the same things, then we might as well all be dead because the joy of life would not exist. There are some countries on this planet which are still considered to be predominantly homogenous. However, that homogeneity is a part of the diversity and contrast of this planet, and within that homogeneity there is contrast as well. Without homogeneity, we would not be able to experience that which is its opposite. There is such beauty in contrast.

The Beauty of Contrast

Abraham teaches that we are non-physical energy, and part of us comes into the physical to explore contrast. When you decided to come forth into this time-space reality, you were so excited about the contrast that would be placed before you. Because in the realm of pure positive energy there is no contrast. It is all love. It is all pure positive energy and straight up connectedness to all that is. So why would you come forth to experience anything other than that? Because there is nothing like the feeling of knowing what you don't want and then knowing what you do want and lining up with that. There is nothing like the feeling of desire and then the path to the fulfilment of that desire. That is life. That is Life! Doesn't a delicious meal feel ever more delicious after you have not eaten for a few hours? Doesn't a shower feel so good after you have been sweating during a workout? Doesn't a nice warm bed feel so wonderful, soft and comfortable after having a long day? You cannot know the sweet without the bitter. You cannot know the hot without the cold. And you know what? It doesn't matter if you prefer hot or cold or bitter or sweet, and even more importantly, it doesn't matter what someone else prefers. You are all here to create your own reality in this beautiful contrasting environment, and the Universe is abundant and willing to fulfil your every desire. It is not possible for you to deprive one another.

But My Parents Deprived Me

It may be true that you were born into an environment in which your parents deprived you of many things. However, you were born whole and worthy and remain whole and worthy throughout your entire life journey despite what you choose to do or not do. This statement, believe it or not, includes your parents. They too were born whole and worthy, despite the choices that they made and or continue to make. You may have been deprived by your parents, but all beings, young and old, can create according to their vibration. Your power to create through your vibration cannot be taken away from you, no matter what obstacles are placed before your path.

Your parents may have been unsupportive, neglectful, or abusive, but you have the power to change your point of attraction. Those days of extreme and uncomfortable contrast have caused you shoot what Abraham calls, *rockets of desire*, for improvement: desires for improved circumstances, better treatment, and an improved environment. As a spiritual being, you knew that this contrast would serve you in that it would cause you to ask for great things which you knew that you could hone through your vibration.

But I didn't know about vibration- I was Just a Kid!

You are not being blamed for not knowing about vibration. Part of your experience upon this planet is to remember that you are vibration. Your contrasting experiences serve as your beginnings and basis for the rockets of desire that shoot forth from you for the rest of your days on this planet. And whether you realized it or not, as a young being, you were learning ways to feel good and find joy despite your surrounding circumstances, because your Inner Being knew and still knows that you have the power to feel good despite what goes on around you.

Have you ever heard of those people whom the masses consider to have reached greatness or have achieved some sort of celebrity status but were born into horrific circumstances? These creators on a spiritual level realized that this horrific contrast would serve them, because in great contrast, there is great asking and great desire. And in great asking and great desire, there is the potential for equally great and dramatic creation. See these creators as your personal evidence that you too can accomplish great things or even greater things. They are teachers. And you are a teacher, whether or not you acknowledge yourself to be so.

You are a Teacher

You are a teacher at the deepest depths of your being; otherwise, you would not be remotely interested in reading a book like this. And the best way to teach is through the power of your example. Be all that you wish to be through your power of focus, and others will watch you and feel inspired by the greatness which you have successfully and personally achieved. The best thing you can do for yourself or anyone else is to get happy. Find your Joy. Follow Your Bliss. Love Yourself. Be the Love in Action that You are and Who you were Born to Be. This is how you serve others. For anything less than this does not serve anyone. You are best to serve yourself and work on yourself so that you, through your example of living a joyous and prosperous life, inspire others to find within themselves the wherewithal to do the same.

You teach through the power of your example, and with this being so, it is worth it to ask yourself: What am I teaching? Am I teaching Joy? Am I teaching fear? Am I teaching scarcity? Am I teaching frustration? Am I teaching Prosperity? Am I teaching Love? How you are feeling right now and how you are predominantly feeling will be the answer to these questions. This is not meant to condemn negative emotion. Bless negative emotion for the signal and guidance that it gives you about where you currently are vibrating, and therefore, attracting. Bless negative emotion because it is a signal that you temporarily got off track and that you can easily go right back on track. It is not a big deal. The shift is not a big deal, nor is where you are a big deal- because it is just at temporary manifestation of a temporary vibration. Your manifestation and physical reality will change as soon as your vibration steadily changes to a new frequency. And you have the wherewithal and power to change your vibration through focus. Through consistent practicing of focusing on what you want, you become the teacher that you came forth to be.

Be That Which You Want to be a Teacher Of

If you want to be a teacher of Love, then do your best to radiate where love is. That means, appreciate and love yourself first and foremost. For then, and only then, will you be in a place to love others from a space of wholeness. If you want to be a teacher of prosperity, go there in your mind to where that prosperous You resides. It does not matter if you have a negative balance in your bank account. If you keep going into your Vortex where the wealthy you resides and go there frequently enough so that you believe in its coming, the abundance will shower all over you and your current negative bank balance will be a memory of the past of who you used to be. It is not your job to figure out the details of how it will come. This is why humans make such a big deal about their problems: they think that they are responsible for moving mountains in order for their problems to be solved, financial or otherwise. That is not how it works. You can try to move mountains, but you will only be met with discouragement and frustration. Go there in your mind where you want to be, and the Universe will light your trail up for you. Then and only then can you be that which you want to be a teacher of.

Your Vortex of Creation

It is ever so beneficial for us to once again revisit the subject of your vortex of creation. A vortex is a pre-manifestational place where the vibration of all that we want to be, do, and have is already in existence in present time-space reality. And once we line up with our Vortex, the things which we are wanting will manifest into physical reality. Your Vortex is where all of your money is, your lovers are, your beautiful new homes, your children, your new and improved bodily condition, and everything that you have imagined or asked for whether it is knowingly or unknowingly. All day, every day we are asking for a variety of things even if we do not consciously know that we are asking. When we are sitting in traffic we are asking for clearer routes for transportation. When we are experiencing a flight delay we are asking for a better airline or better customer service, and so on. So when we line up with the same vibration of Source, that is, the vibration where the feeling of love, bliss, passion, and knowing reside, we are inside of our Vortex of creation and the manifestations happen quite quickly and almost instantaneously.

Your Vortex includes all that you have chosen from the variety that surrounds you. So there is no need to be concerned about the variety that surrounds us. As Abraham often says, we are chefs working in a kitchen with every ingredient imaginable. Just because there is Tabasco sauce in the kitchen does not mean that you have to use it for your pie unless you want to. However, your attention to the Tabasco sauce will eventually get into your pie. All that you are giving your attention to will get into your pie. So it is best not to pay attention or focus upon those ingredients that you do not want, as this behaviour will spit you out of your Vortex. Just pick the things you want and focus on those, and then you will be able to make the pie that is most pleasing to you. Your attention to it puts it in your pie. Attention to what you really want helps to get you into your Vortex of creation. Contrast need not be something to guard against.

Contrast is Variety-That's It!

Contrast is simply variety. What is considered to be the mean, bad and the ugly to you may not be considered to be mean, bad and ugly to others. A variety of things that may be pleasing to people depending upon where they currently vibrate on what Abraham calls the *emotional scale*. This is the scale of emotions which ranges from powerlessness to bliss, and it includes everything in between. Have you ever had the experience of being angry at someone and then encountering someone else who is also angry about something similar (maybe they also were cheated by the same person), and the two of you complain about it together? Doesn't that feel good? Those moments feel good because at that moment, you are expressing your anger and enjoying the downstream expression of your anger, because previously you may have been feeling powerless or revenge, so anger is a better feeling place for you. What Abraham advises however, is to not stay there too long, because if you stay in the mode of anger you will continue to attract from that angry space. It is important to stay for only as long as it feels good to you, and when it no longer feels good you will soon realize that a place of less anger, or frustration, is the better feeling place that you are looking for. From there, soon enough you will feel better in a place of hope. And when you are in a place of hope, you will soon be having access to your Vortex. It really is that simple. Just reach for the better feeling thought from wherever you stand, and always follow and honor your inner guidance in the process, and soon you will be feeling better again. It is the only thing that you can do, and it is the best thing you can do, and it is enough. That is all you need to do: just reach for a better feeling thought, and then another, and then another, for as long as it feels comfortable to do so. When it stops being comfortable, just let it go. You may even try to say to yourself, "I'll just let it go for now. I am just going to let go of this resistance as best as I can and give it to the Universe to handle the details." You will be surprised by how well this works. Not only does it help you to feel relief (however slight or big it may be), but you will soon find yourself able to be open or even distracted by something that is brighter and more beautiful, which will bring you swiftly into the Vortex. The contrast, while it includes many unwanted things which cause you negative emotion when you focus upon them, can and does serve you. It makes your Vortex ever more bright, bountiful, and beautiful. The contrast helps you to choose all of the details of what you want. This is the abundant platform that a deliberate creator longs for!

Chapter 4 : Set Your Own Table

Setting the Table of Your Life is such a fun and creative endeavour. It is also an activity that reminds you that You are the Creator of Your own Life Experience- and that is a good thing, because you can include all of the wonderful things that are most important and pleasurable for YOU!

By setting the table of your life, you can choose the type of plates, silverware, napkins, tablecloth, flowers, and anything else you may want to include. It could be as simple or as elaborate as you want it to be. The main point is that you are making all of the choices on your own. There is no one else involved in the process of setting your own table. When you set the table of your life experience, you can choose the friends, the type of activities, the types of places you go to, and virtually just about anything (except family!) that is pleasing to you. When it comes to family, on a spiritual, non-physical level, you do choose the family you are born into, as you knew that the contrast that the family you chose would serve you in your creating. And as always, contrast helps you to define and focus upon what it is that you want.

Make a List of All of the Things You Want

Make a list of all the things that you want and look at it every day, or as frequently as you remember to do so. If you forget a day it is okay. However, it is very valuable to make it a habit to ask yourself what it is that you want and why you want it on a daily basis and as often as you can throughout the day, because we are ever evolving, changing beings, and as we change, our wants change. We are eternally amending our desires and dreaming new dreams- it is the natural way for a human being to experience life. Because of our evolving nature it is important to ask ourselves what we want, for what we wanted yesterday may not be what we want today. The contrast of yesterday's experience will have either caused you to amend or amplify your desire, so it is always wonderful to get into the habit of checking in with your Self on a regular basis. It is important to consistently and daily focus upon what you want, as this focus will draw those things into your experience.

Focus on What You Want and Ignore What You Don't Want

Focusing on what you want and ignoring what you don't want is much easier said that done. However, with practice, you will eventually get it. As with any skill such as playing the piano or learning how to ice skate, you will make mistakes along the way, and you may feel frustration. But with focus, you eventually will see the evidence and result of your focusing powers.

It is most important to focus on how and what the experience or desired circumstance or object *feels* like. Remember the goodness of the feeling. Remember the excitement of the acquisition of the desired situation. It is the feeling that is the most important element. Everything else is just detail. When you can feel your manifestation- what it looks like, what it sounds like, what it tastes like, what it smells like, what it feels like, then you are using your creative focusing powers to your advantage. When you are able to viscerally feel your manifestation consistently, you will be surprised by how fast you align with your desire. It is the feeling that is the indicator of your proximity to your Vortex and how close or how far you are from all that you desire.

Focus as often as you can on what you do want. If you start to give your attention to what you don't want, or to the contrasting experience that caused you to ask for improvement, then you are mixing your vibration with both wanted and unwanted. And when you mix your vibration with wanted and unwanted, the Universe cannot yield to you those things that you want, for your vibration is not purely focused. When you catch yourself focusing on what you don't want, or focusing upon things that do not make you feel good, be kind to yourself and pivot your thoughts in the direction of what you are wanting. You may try saying to yourself, "Oh yes. I forgot. I'm glad that my awareness is increasing and that I am able to stop myself in the middle of an unproductive thought. Now I will simply focus on what I want. No big deal." Being kind to yourself during your learning process is the key, because being hard on yourself is counterproductive to receiving that which you desire.

Be as specific or as general as feels good to you. You can be as general as saying, "I want each and every day to be as joyous as possible, and it doesn't matter how it unfolds," or you can be as specific as stating the exact details that are most pleasing to you. What is most important is that the process feels good, feels comfortable, and feels easy-going. It can be as easy as asking yourself, "What colour table cloth would I like for my table?"

What's Your Favourite Colour?

Besides the fact that colour has a magical and impervious power behind it, it is so important to lavish yourself with your favourite colours when setting your table. For it is your unique and individual creation and expression of your personality and preferences. There is such pleasure to be had when placing your gaze upon colours that please you in your home, dress, belongings, food, and face (if you wear make-up). The pleasure that you will feel is the magic that only beauty can provide- beauty that is uniquely judged by you to be beautiful and worthy of the utmost praise. In setting your own table you get to choose what suits you, what feels best for you, what feels right for you, what looks best on you, and what looks best around you. By using your favourite colours you are affirming that you are the artist of your experience, the genius creator that is in touch with the palate that is most pleasurable for you and only you.

Chapter 5: Turn off the Telly & Turn on Your Inner Movie Theatre

Turn off the frequencies and vibrations of others that are force-fed to your through your television, and create your own reality through the powerful images of things that you want in your own mind-your inner movie theatre.

Turn off your television and take some time to visualize all that you desire. The more attention that you give to all that you desire, the sooner it will be your experience. There is so much information, opinions, and scandals streaming through your television, being forced in your direction. From the latest disease to the latest infidelity, the media is constantly trying to manipulate your thoughts into getting what they want from you and convincing you to conform your actions to meet their desires, and more importantly, their bottom line. While there are some truly beneficial television programs on the air today, many exist as entertainment geared towards getting you to buy or subscribe to what suits the network's needs.

It is important to monitor how you feel when you watch a certain programme, which means bringing your focus back onto your needs, rather than the needs of the companies who created the programme you are watching. Ask yourself, "How do I feel right now as I watch this? Am I feeling good, or am I feeling bad?" Oftentimes we make the excuse to watch something to be informed, even though the information makes us feel bad. You must be self-loving enough to care about how you feel at any given moment of the day, even when watching television. The time that people watch television is a prime time period where most people who want to be deliberate creators sort of go blank. They forget that even when watching television, they need to be aware of how they feel. It is amazing what can happen during the minutes or hours of vibrational air time of watching a television programme. For example, a person can go from a feeling range of okay to good prior to watching television, and if they 'zone out' as most people do when they watch television, and lose awareness about the way that they feel, the programme can help them go from an okay to good feeling place, to one that is worse! It happens all too frequently, and it is important to either be aware of how a television programme makes you feel, or just turn off the television all together. You can feed yourself with entertainment that does make you feel good. It is a matter of choice. It is a matter of choosing what you want to create.

It is difficult to create what you want when you are continuously being stuffed with other people's ideas which have absolutely nothing to do with manifesting your dreams. It is important to focus on programmes that feel good to you and which move you towards that which you are wanting. Even if the programme has nothing to do with your future desires but makes you feel good, you know then that it is a good programme for you. For when you are feeling good, you are heading towards, or allowing all that it is that you want. It is the feeling that is most important. Turn off the telly and turn on your inner movie theatre, and you will see how this positively affects your life.

What is My Inner Movie Theatre?

Your inner movie theatre is the collection of beautiful images and scenarios which you alone create in your mind either during your visualization processes, day dreams, or meditations. These are images of the things that you desire for yourself and maybe for others. They are the images of what you desire to be, do, and have. They are the images of the circumstances which you wish to experience. The movie that plays in your mind is completely up to you. You get to choose what it looks like and how the story unfolds. It is of such great value to turn most of your attention to the images of your inner movie theatre because these are the images of your purest desire, and focusing on them will attract them into your current reality all the more sooner. As long as the images and the movie feels good to you, then playing your movie will help to move you swiftly towards that which you are wanting. Your inner movie theatre is way more important than any outside source of entertainment. It is your personal creation made by your Inner Being in connection with Source Energy. It is the movie you create through seeing your world through the eyes of Source.

Seeing Your World through the Eyes of Your Divine Self

When you remember Who You Really Are and see your world through the eyes of your divine and total self, everything is wonderful and magical, even if it is ugly by other people's standards. Your Divine Self is an expert at spotting beauty all around your environment and is well practiced at focusing your gaze on things that you like and love. Your divine self appreciates the colours in the sky, the temperature of the air, the brilliance of the sky during the transition from daytime to night time, the sounds in the environment, the laughter of other humans, the sound of your own voice, and the beauty and perfection of all that is. It notices the flight of a bird, the purring of a cat, the barking of a dog, the wagging of its tail, the smell of freshly baked cookies in the air, the fresh smell of a newly washed load of laundry, and the sturdiness of a beautiful antique dining table. The eyes of your divine self appreciates and sees all beauty in all things and all beings. Seeing your world through these eyes is the ultimate act of Spiritual Hedonism- pleasuring all of your senses in connection with your divine and total self. It is living your life in a way that you allow Source to move through you and experience through all of your senses the greatness of this Universe. When you create your inner movie through the eyes of Source in this way, you will soon realize and understand the control you have over your life experience.

You Are the Director and the Leading Actor

You are the director of your life through your thoughts, not your actions. You in your physical body are the leading actor. Enjoy your movie, for this movie is your life! Once you leave your physical body it will be obvious to you the perfection of this Universe and how all is just an interpretation of vibration and translated perspective which can easily be changed at any time. You will realize why you chose the character that you did. You will realize why you chose your race, ethnicity, skin colour, heritage, and parents. You will soon understand why you chose to be born into the situation which you were born into. You will come to know how valuable the contrast of your life has been for you and how it provided such fruitful grounds for you as a genius creator of life experience. All of these things will become clear to you. You will understand that you really were the director of your own movie and that you also had the starring role. And even bigger, you will realize that all of it was not a big deal because you knew that you could come back again and be a different actor with a different background and perspective. You will understand your infinite nature as a Divine director of a brilliant and original movie.

This Inner Movie Thing is All Fine and Good, but What About a Day Job?

Source Energy acknowledges the importance of money in most societies and how it is necessary to most human beings' experience of survival. Depending upon where you fall on the emotional scale, and what your current financial situation is, it may very well feel better to keep your day job for now. This statement of course is referring to those who are asking the above question because they are unhappy with their current life situation in reference to work. There is oftentimes a misunderstanding when the lesson of the inner movie is introduced to a new student because it is frequently taken to mean that one must ignore his or her responsibilities and daydream all day. That is not the purpose of the inner movie theatre. It is something that you can turn on at anytime that is convenient for you, just as you would turn on a television when the time is right or when it is convenient.

It does not take much time or effort to increase your daydreaming or visualizing. Just a few minutes a day makes a difference. Make time for it in the evenings and on your days off. Seriously schedule it in. It is one of the most important and loving things you can do for yourself- to make time to be inside of Your Vortex. The more you practice this, the sooner the need for a day job will gradually dissipate (if that is what you prefer), because your pleasure will become your dominant vibration, and activities of pleasure that also generate dollars will replace what you are currently experiencing and labelling as a day job.

You may want to try having conversations with yourself such as this to make yourself feel better:

This experience (your day job) is all a part of the creative process. I created this experience out of my past beliefs about how money should flow, and I will do my best to enjoy every moment to the best of my ability. The people with whom I am interacting with: clients, co-workers, supervisors, etc. are also co-creators in this experience and deep down we all want the same things: freedom, growth, and joy. I am just going to relax and enjoy my interactions with them, because I know that this is all temporary and soon enough I will not be sharing my space with these people- they will be a part of my past and who I used to be. So for now, I will just say, 'My new future experience is moulding and shifting and is on its way to me, and in the meantime, I will extend appreciation for the good things about where I am and who I am this day. It's all good, and I trust in the Universe to mould my future experience to be filled with delicious things. I am going to be easy with myself regarding what I have created which I am experiencing right now. I love myself, and I know that I just did the best that I could with what I knew then, which has resulted in my now. And I'm not going to make a big deal about where I am now because I know that where I am now is just a temporary manifestation on the way to where I really want to be. Every single person who I look up to and admire has experienced the same exact feeling that I am feeling now: not being completely satisfied with where they are and wishing that things could be different. But now I am wiser because I know that the better I get at relaxing about where I am, trusting that my desires are on their way, and appreciating the good things about my current reality, the closer my future reality will take shape and form and manifest into the physical. It's cool where I am and where I am going is much cooler. Where I am going is much brighter and more beautiful than my here and now. I am really, really looking forward to where I am going.

I am actually starting to feel excitement about where I am going. I love looking at where I am headed, because it feels so darn good. I can't wait to get there, but I can wait to get there at the same time! Life is good and getting better and better every day. I love being a deliberate creator. It is so much fun!'

Visualizing for the Fun of Visualizing

Many new students of the *Law of Attraction*, also called the *Art of Allowing*, tend to use the process of visualizing in a way that is a bit strict and in the spirit of trying too hard. If it feels like work, then it is work, so there is no point to it if it feels difficult. The reason why there is no point to it is because the whole purpose of the process of visualization is to have fun and feel light, free, and frisky. That is the vibration of the Vortex. The point is to get you to see what is inside of your Vortex. If it's not fun or does not feel good-don't do it. The point of it is to feel good and to get yourself into alignment. Anything less than that is going in the wrong direction!

Chapter 6: Mix Only with the Best

You are a Child of Divine Energy- don't you know that you were born deserving the Best? It doesn't matter whether or not you were born into the Best, what matters is that you KNOW that You were born DESERVING. Whether or not other people think you are deserving is irrelevant. You were born KNOWING that you could create the best even if it did not currently surround you.

Mix only with the best that you can comfortably afford and envision for yourself in the place that you are standing in right now, here in this moment. The better you become at making peace with where you are and what you have right now, the greater your life experience will become. For in that vibration of being at peace with what is, no matter what is going on around you, you place yourself into the receiving mode of that which you are wanting. Mix with the best that you have access to right now and praise it. The more you practice this, the better and better the things you will have access to will become, and your idea of 'best' will get greater and greater, higher and higher. It is Universal Law. You are where you are, and where you are is just fine- no matter what other people outside of you will label it to be. Where you are right now is between You and Your Source anyway- no one else or nothing else is relevant to the improvement of your life experience except for your relationship with You, your relationship with Source, your relationship with your Inner Being.

Allow Your Standards to Rise

A lot of times when you are on a journey towards enlightenment or self-fulfilment, the people around you may start to annoy you. And the people around you become annoying, largely because you are going through deliberate growth, and they have stayed the same. It is during this time of growth when you have raised your standards, that people may annoy you, because while you have grown the standards of the people around you may have stayed the same. Allow your standards to rise anyway. Do not fear the parting of those who are not growing at the same rate as you. For in holding on to your past, even if holding onto your past means holding onto your yesterday, you are holding yourself back. The Universe is abundant and will bring you new people and new relationships which are a true reflection of your higher standards and what you are now wanting from your new vantage point. Let the present and the past drift away naturally, and watch what unfolds as you allow yourself to be raised into a higher dimension.

Do Your Best, Be Your Best, Then Let It Go

Don Miguel Ruiz in his book, *The Four Agreements*, describes this process beautifully, so beautifully that it is worth it to mention it again and again. When you do your best in any situation, it is easy to let go, because you have a feeling of completion. You have a feeling of, "OK, I've done all that I can do and I can do no more." Or, the thought of doing more feels worse than the thought of letting it go. Again, this is the practice of what Abraham often refers to as asking yourself what feels better or what feels worse. Does it feel better to go to the bank today, or does it feel better to wait until first thing tomorrow morning? Does it feel better to pay my bill now while I remember, or does it feel better to wait? Does it feel better to do my laundry tonight, or does it feel better to wait until the weekend? These simple decisions make a difference in the overall quality of your day-to-day life. If you feel that you have done your best today, it is easy to decide whether you should do something today or to wait until a better time. Again, there is no right or wrong, but there is a relativity of what feels worse or what feels better.

Oftentimes many people take this to mean that doing their best means getting as much done as they can in any given day. But Abraham teaches that humans try too hard to get leverage through their behaviour and action. Accomplishing a long list of things in one day through various actions usually does not feel good, because an overload of action, especially action while not in alignment with Source Energy, is exhausting. And exhaustion does not feel good. People usually tend to their vibration last, which is the most important thing to tend to in order to manifest and create that which they are wanting. For lining up vibration is far more powerful than any action one can perform. When you act through inspiration, through a strong impulse from your Inner Being to do something, then that action is extremely powerful. Action taken from the impulse of inspiration is action that is in alignment with Source Energy, and action taken from that standpoint can create far more than countless actions taken while out of alignment. By doing your best, your best meaning doing what feels best to you at any given time, you are serving yourself and others. Do what feels best to you in any given moment, and you will truly be in alignment with the Universe.

Allow the Universe to Handle the Details

When you ask, it is given, so let the Universe do its work on your behalf. It is impossible from your human-mind perspective to orchestrate the people, events, timing, and circumstances to make something happen, so just let it go. It is not your job, and you couldn't do it even if you tried. Let the Universe handle the details. Your job is to ask, and your job is to desire, and the Universe's job is to answer. There is a beauty in the balance of that. To take control and do the orchestration yourself is defying the laws of the Universe, and whenever you get yourself worked up from this type of standpoint things don't work out anyway, and at best the results are mediocre. Leave it to the Universe, leave it to Source, or leave it to God. It does not matter what you call it. Practice trusting the process little by little and soon enough you will understand that this truly does work.

I Know I Deserve the Best and I'm Excited Because the Best is Now Coming to Me!

If you know that you are worthy and deserving then you have conquered half of the battle, because your thoughts are in alignment with what Your Source is thinking about you. If you are currently having problems knowing about your worthiness and deservingness, then practice thoughts of self-love and self-appreciation on a daily, regular basis. Put yourself on a regimine if need be, and you can do so even if you are not having problems with worthiness issues. Make a promise to yourself to say, "I Love You," to yourself the first thing when you wake up in the morning and the last thing you do before you fall asleep at night. Make a practice of saying it to yourself in all moments of fear or anxiety you may experience throughout the day. You may want to add, "I Love You, and you are my best friend. Let's relax because we have each other to get through this. This is just temporary and it will pass soon." Being your own best friend will work wonders for you and your self esteem, self confidence, and it will surely increase your self-worth. To know that you are deserving, and having the feeling of positive expectation, are the key ingredients for manifesting your heart's desires. When you practice loving yourself more and more each day, it will become easier and natural to expect the best.

Chapter 7: Stop Staring at the Oven Waiting for the Bread to Rise

If you KNEW the inevitability of manifesting all of your desires, you would never feel an ounce of impatience. For you would know that the Universe operates upon its own schedule and is just waiting for you to line up with it through maintaining a vibration of delicious joy. Your Daily Bread is ensured-expect it to rise and it will.

It is easier to be patient when you know that something is on its way to you and that in a short time it will be at your door. The more you practice *knowing* that the thing that you want is on its way, the less you are likely to get so upset that it is not there yet. This is what it means to stop staring at the oven waiting for the bread to rise.

When one bakes a loaf of bread, he or she follows instructions which they either read or which were passed down to them and committed to memory. First, they preheat the oven, next, they mix the ingredients together, then, they knead the dough, and eventually when all is complete they put the dough in the oven to bake. If they are a first time baker, they may worry a bit about whether or not they followed the instructions properly and may question how the loaf of bread will turn out. But they have faith and are willing to give it a chance. Even if they forgot an ingredient and the loaf of bread does not turn out as planned, it is not a big deal, because they can remember to add the forgotten ingredient next time and try again.

If they are an experienced baker and have used this recipe and process many times, they will not doubt that the bread will bake and rise, as it has every other time. There is no reason to feel worry, anxiety, or stress that the process does not happen instantaneously. With a little faith, they know that in due time the loaf of bread will be done and ready to eat.

This is a similar process for all of creation. If you mould your energies into better feeling places, in time, you will manifest that which you desire. If this is your first time doing this, there is no need to worry. Everyone starts somewhere and everyone was once a beginner at something at some point in their lives. Most humans are socialized to create through action. They are socialized to take steps that they are told to take, follow instructions they are told to follow, and do as they are told to do. Source Energy does not deny that action can and does lead to creation. In fact, in the previous example, baking bread takes some action steps. However, what Abraham teaches is that there is a huge difference between inspired action, action taken from a wonderful feeling place that feels like it cannot be avoided, and action that is taken from a frustrated, 'I have to do this thing' feeling-state.

Have you ever eaten food created without love? Doesn't it taste bad, or mediocre at best? It is difficult to tell the difference between good food and bad food if you are so hungry that discernment may not play a big role in your state of mind when only being fed does. However, if the same bad tasting dish were eaten immediately before a dish made with love, it would be obvious what the difference tastes like. The one made with love will have been made on an entirely different level. The person who made the dish connected to Source will have naturally utilized the best temperatures, the right seasoning, and served it at just the right time. The one made without love would have had been made by someone who just threw a bunch of ingredients together, and while they may be the right ingredients, the dish just didn't turn out right. There is a huge difference between creations made while in the flow or going with the current and those that are created against the flow, or resisting the current. There is magic that happens when you act in inspiration, going with the flow of life, and connected to Source Energy. All of your actions taken and performed under these conditions produce an extraordinary outcome as opposed to a mediocre or bad one.

When you do your best, no matter where you stand on the emotional scale, you are in the flow of life. When you do your best, it is easy to let go, and let things be. It is easy to allow things to happen, because there is a peace of mind that comes with knowing that you have done all that you can do, and that is enough. One thing that is helpful to do when you are caught in a web of feeling worried or anxious is to ask yourself, "Have I done everything that I can do?" And if the answer is 'yes,' then just let it go. Not that action is always the answer-sometimes it is contradictory to taking you towards the answer. However, by following your inner guidance, your gut, your feeling, you will be able to know if you have done enough. And once you have determined that you have done enough, just let it go. Stop watching the oven waiting for the bread to rise. Once you have taken all of the steps that you feel at peace with taking, let the Universe handle the details. Let the oven do its job. Let the yeast do the rising for you. Let go of the need to control that which you cannot control and that which is not your job. You will save yourself so much time and energy in doing so, and this time and energy can be spent enjoying your life, rather than worrying about it.

Look for the Evidence that Surrounds You, Because it is Everywhere

Oftentimes it is easier to see evidence of the *Law of Attraction* in other people's lives before we can see the evidence of it in our own. The reason for this is because we have very little to no resistance when it comes to others' desires because they do not have much of an impact on our personal lives in the same way that our own desires do. The resistance factor is dramatically different. Use this to your advantage. See the evidence in other people's life circumstances if it helps you to believe in the laws for yourself. Look at the people in your life that you know fairly well, and watch and see how their thoughts and feelings line up with their manifestations. Look at their relationships, their finances, and the overall way that they live their lives. Through simple observation of those around you, it will be easy to find evidence of the *Law of Attraction* at work. When you mentally gather this evidence, it will be easier to understand that there is a universal timing to manifestation. That universal timing is alignment of thought coupled with a vibration of expectation. There is no need to watch the bread bake in the oven. If you took all of the steps you could to make a good loaf, the bread will rise on its own, whether or not you stand there and stare at it.

When It's Time, You'll KNOW

When you know, you KNOW. The feeling will be undeniable. It's like the feeling that you have when you need to go to the bathroom. You don't really take much time to think about it, analyze it, or ponder it. You know that you have to go because the feeling is clear and undeniable. This is how strong the impulse will be when it is time. The impulse will viscerally feel too strong to ignore. You always have the choice to ignore it, but ignoring it will be too painful, and oftentimes people cannot stand the feeling of the pain of ignoring it, so they just go. If you procrastinate long enough, you will have to make that decision of, "Am I willing to put up with the pain of not going, or should I just go to ease this pain? Going feels so much better, and soon enough I won't have a choice." This not having a choice bit is what happens when the Universe sort of pushes you in the direction of what you really want. It is the choice of going downstream, with the flow of life. Sometimes that forcing or pushing you in that direction will translate into being laid off from your job, your lover leaving you, not getting the job, or being rejected from that audition. These circumstances are really blessings in disguise when you take the time to see them from your future standpoint and from a place of alignment with Source. During the time that these things are happening they may feel painful, but in hindsight, these circumstances are all cooperative components in making the timing just right for you and your rendezvous with other co-creators who have something to give you towards your desires and future experiences. It is important to remind yourself of Who You Really Are: non-physical energy which has come forth into a physical body, to experience this environment of contrast called, 'Life'.

Instead of Patience, Practice Knowing

Some of you may be sick and tired of hearing the proverb, "Patience is a virtue," and may often say to yourself, "I've been waiting my whole damn life for this. How much more patient can I get?" If this is the way that you feel, it is a good idea to practice *knowing*, rather than patience.

Knowing, is the visceral place where you know that you are Source Energy in a physical body. It is feeling the reality of that. It is knowing that through your breath, you have life on this physical plane, and that which makes you breathe is connected to all that is, all that you want, and all that you want to rendezvous with. It is understanding with full comprehension that you are already connected to that which you want. Your only job is to release the resistance you have which is currently holding it apart from you.

Knowing is understanding that through your living of life that you have accumulated much resistance, most of it unknowingly, because it is likely that you simple acclimated to your environment more than you spent time visualizing the environment, circumstances, and situations that you want. Knowing is feeling okay about that and understanding that all that is can easily change. It is understanding in your gut that your current reality is just temporary. It is understanding that the Universe has the ability to orchestrate people, circumstances, and events, and that it is not your job to do so. Your job is to learn how to feel good. Your job is to know that feeling good is your divine birth right. It is knowing that feeling good means acting out of self-love and choosing out of self-love. Knowing does not need patience, because one who knows understands that the request has been answered. One who knows understands that the deed has been done. All it takes is allowing things to be, relaxing, and expecting its arrival. A person, who knows, expects. A person who knows expects things to go well and expects all of their wishes and dreams to come true. Practice knowing, first by knowing Who You Really Are, and then the rest will come naturally.

Chapter 8: Say a Prayer of Thanks

Appreciation is an energy that creates an atmosphere of positivity for yourself and those around you. This energy is the exact breeding ground for manifesting your desires and helping others to manifest theirs.

Living a life of appreciation can be one of the most delicious and powerful ways to go about having a life experience. As you practice the art of appreciation, your vibration soars to great heights. When you really get good at it, you will learn to even appreciate the perceived injustices you have experienced for the lessons you have learned and the growth you have experienced because of them.

The Power of Appreciation

There is such a magical power behind thoughts of appreciation. Appreciation is your Self in alignment with Source, for Source walks around all day, every day in appreciation. When you are in a vibration of appreciation, you are seeing your world through the eyes of Source. There is such power in that.

Seeing the world through the eyes of Source is almost exactly the same way babies and very young toddlers see the world. Have you ever seen a young child point at the moon and shout, "Moon!" so excited by its mere existence and shining light warming up the night sky with its beautiful glow. This is just a glimpse of what it is like to see the world through the eyes of source. There is a power in the appreciation of the simple beauty of things we take for granted. Appreciating the beauty that surrounds you is a fast way to get into your Vortex, and consistently doing so will help you to open to receive your desires in a swift and enjoyable way.

Shifting Your Vibration through Appreciation

When you take your focus off of what you don't want and take the time to compliment something or appreciate something that you like or love, you have shifted your vibration towards manifesting something that you want. For you cannot focus on something negative or unwanted and appreciate at the same time. This shift in attention is a shifting of your vibration into a positive direction.

Even in the most dire of circumstances there is always something that you can find to appreciate. Even if you think it is absolutely impossible to find something to appreciate, you can always appreciate that you are breathing. You can appreciate that your body hasn't given up on you and that it always does its job of providing you with oxygen to keep you alive without you having to say or do anything about it. You don't command your body to do its job, it just does it. You don't have to bribe your heart to beat or your lungs to fill up with air. You don't have to exert any power or influence over your nerves for them to let you know when you have touched a hot stove or when you are in a cold environment and need to put on a jacket. Your body just does its divine natural job on its own. Isn't that a miracle in and of itself? It doesn't matter where you are or what you are currently experiencing. So what if you can't pay the bills this month- you're breathing! Your heart is beating and your lungs are working and so long as that is all good, the answers to how you will pay your bills will come. Appreciate the now, and keep on appreciating, and all things will truly work themselves out at the right time. Appreciation is walking in the direction of who you really are and who you intended to be before you decided to inhabit this physical body. Appreciation is one of the fastest ways of changing your vibration. By making a habit of appreciating, you will soon be observing an entirely new life experience. It will be as if all of the things that used to worry you will naturally melt away. It is something that you can practice to change your life in a big way.

Chapter 9: Indulge & Savour Every Moment of Your Creation!

Life is supposed to be delicious, and life is supposed to be good. You were meant to go from one creation to the next, enjoying every step of the way! Congratulate Yourself on every creation, because every creation is of your own doing, and it is evidence of your power. Your POWER is most definitely something to indulge and savour!

One of the most valuable things that you can do for yourself is to acknowledge that much of what you are living right now was once a dream. It was once a thought that you were not lined up with but then practiced getting into vibrational alignment with. Everything around you is a manifestation of your thought. Congratulate yourself! You created it! Isn't that a wonderful thing? You can create more of what you want, or change the state of some current manifestations. You can make the decision today to be more deliberate in your creations. Each moment is a new moment to begin again. It does not matter what you have created up until now, because Source Energy accepts all creations in a non-judgemental manner and just routes for your joy and for your recognition of your power to create all of the things that you are wanting. It is only a matter of changing your vibration, and you are constantly shooting off new rockets of desire whether you realize that you are or not, so you might as well enjoy the process! Enjoying and savouring the process serves you well, because it puts you into a better feeling place, which creates the vibration that will bring to you all of your desires.

Journaling, Photography, and Scrapbooking

Journaling, photographing, and scrapbooking your everyday life will help you to consciously appreciate life's moments on a deeper level. By engaging in one or all of these activities on a regular basis, you will begin to realize how special moments happen on seemingly ordinary days. However, they pass you by when you fail to acknowledge or notice them.

When you act as if your life is a series of precious moments, you immediately bring yourself into the awareness of the temporary nature of this life and how beautiful and wonderful it is and can be. When you take pictures on a vacation and place them in your scrapbook, aren't you predominantly feeling appreciation and joy for the wonderful experiences you had on your journey? Well, all of life is a journey.

And all of it can be special and important if you allow yourself to see it that way. All of it can be beautiful and worthy of taking a picture of and revealing over and remembering. The physical action of recording your daily life and daily events will truly help you to understand the precious moments this life has to offer you on a daily basis.

Maintaining regular memories of yourself for you to look back upon can serve you greatly throughout your life. The physical reminders of pictures, ticket stubs, notes, or anything else you may collect along the way to include in one of your journals or scrapbooks, help you to remember where you have been, where you have come from, and how life has changed in comparison to where you are headed. These mementos will also serve as a reminder to you that life really can be and is an adventure vacation from the pure non-physical realm.

Life as an Adventure Vacation

Oftentimes it is helpful to close your eyes for a few minutes and put your mind in a place where you are thinking or planning a vacation. It can be any type of vacation you want such as a twelve cities in ten days bus tour, or a relaxing resort-style break. There really is no right or wrong. Then open your eyes and realize that the process of all of your life is just like this. On your vacation you go from one place to another, have different meals, taste different food, go to different places, transport your body from one place to another using different modes of transportation, take pictures, talk, walk, play, laugh, see, experience, and so on. In essence, all of your life is an adventure vacation of your own creation. Remind yourself of this on a regular basis, and it will help you to create in the direction of the adventure vacation you are looking to experience.

Even that which you call 'work' is a part of your adventure vacation. For when planning a vacation, are you not spending time planning the journey, your activities, taking care of the practical things such as paying for your plane ticket, contacting the cab company, paying for gas, and arranging the details of your accommodation? The difference between these activities and the activities which many refer to as, 'work,' or 'my job' is the perception of those activities. The popular belief is that the former are performed with the result of having a good time, while the latter are performed out of duty or obligation to get paid. While Source Energy acknowledges that humans do create commitments and experience what they call 'obligations', Source Energy also acknowledges that they make far too big of a deal out of all of it. Over time, performing these everyday activities can become less of a struggle or burden and more of a non-issue and even a pleasure for some. By focusing upon the positive aspects of anything, you release your resistance to the well-being that is your inheritance. And when you do so, the Universe accommodates you in ways that will bring more joy to all of your daily activities, to the point that the concept of obligation is no longer much of a part of your experience. For these feelings of, "I have to," will subside and will be replaced with more feelings of, "I want to because I will feel better if I do." With enough practice, you can and will truly experience life as the adventure vacation that it is- laundry, bills, and all!

Enjoy This Moment, because the Manifestation Process is About to Begin-Again!

The life of a deliberate creator is endless and continuous- it is eternal. You explore contrast, decide what you want and what you don't want. Then you line up with what you do want and then manifestation occurs. Now you are in a new vibrational vantage point. And in this new vantage point there is new contrast. And the process starts over again. You decide from your new vantage point what you want and what you don't want. So enjoy this moment because the cycle is eternal, and with practice this eternal cycle can be one of pure joy. As Abraham so wonderfully points out, "You did not come forth to get it done!" There is nothing that you have to do. The whole point is to experience the joy of creation and the joy of living. The manifestation process is eternal, as you are an eternal being.

Feeing Good As Often and as Regularly as Possible

Savouring every moment is all a part of feeling good as regularly as possible. An example of this is a simple statement of, "I love this ice cream that I am eating. I am so appreciative of the inventors of this flavour- they are such geniuses." Making statements to yourself like this will put you in a state of loving what you are doing in that very moment and appreciating those who helped to make that delicious moment possible. It is experiencing and appreciating pleasure in all of its fine moments.

If you are currently under the weather you can still practice feeling good by saying things like, "I appreciate the makers of this disposable tissue," or, "I appreciate the person who created this handkerchief, it's so soft and useful and is helping me to contribute to helping the environment." You can even try a statement such as, "Even though I feel a bit sick right now, it is nice to be in my cozy, warm bed. I love my blanket." This all may sound silly at first, but simple statements like this have a powerful way of shifting your mood into a better mood, which will in turn bring you closer to your healing as well.

All Is Well- Take Life One Segment at A Time

Abraham teaches the wonderful process of *segment intending* in which they encourage setting an intention(s) for each segment of the day. For instance, one of the first segments of the day is when we awaken, get out of bed, and go to the bathroom. This can be considered one segment in which you can set the intention to arise peacefully and in the most positive state of mind available to you at that moment. Upon waking, you can open your eyes and say to yourself, "I have just re-emerged into this physical life experience. I am appreciative of the sleep and non-physical restoration which I have just received. It is my intention to start my day peacefully and calmly, thinking kinds thoughts about myself and those which whom I will interact with today. I appreciate my bed, my running water, and all of the resources which surround me." This may sound like a dramatic way to start off your first segment of the day, but the more you practice this time of self-talk, you will gradually see the dramatic shifts that will take place in your life experience. You will find yourself savouring life's moments in a deeper and more profound way. You will find yourself seeing the ordinary through the eyes of Source and seeing beauty surrounding you when you previously did not know it was even there. You will gradually let go of any previous anxiety or worry that you used to feel about many things and about many subjects, simply because you are filling your moments of life with ever increasing positive thoughts. You will find a lot of unwanted things melting away or dissipating from your experience because these negative things no longer have room in your life. Now your life is being filled and occupied with wanted situations, people, circumstances, thoughts, and feelings. This savouring your creation process is a way to continuously remind yourself that you are the Creator of your life experience and that no one can vibrate in your experience but you. The more you remind yourself of your personal power, the more you will remember to use it rather than experiencing life by default. Instead of getting your vibration out of wack when someone says something overly critical or unkind to you, you are able to take a moment, feel the negative emotion, and re-direct your thoughts into a more positive direction. You will be able to acknowledge your anger, annoyance, irritation, worry, or fear, and then bless it. You will bless it for the guidance that it gives you, because your guidance is now reminding you that there is a vibrational escrow of all the things that you want that you have temporarily moved away from. Living your life in segments and savouring your creations will put you in a wonderful place of awareness and sensitivity to your Self. Your relationship with your Self will grow stronger and stronger each day you practice this. It will grow to the point where your contact with Self is simply normal, and your communication with your Self will become increasingly clearer and undeniable, enabling you to make choices which are more in alignment with what you are wanting. There is nothing more important than working on your relationship with your Self, for when you are in alignment with Self, everything else in your life manifests so swiftly and smoothly in a fun and delightful way. Manifestations coming from a disconnected from Self place are a struggle- hard, difficult, and oftentimes painful. In the name of Self-Love you must remember as often as you can throughout the day how important and loved you are by Universal Energy. This practice will create such positive and wonderful change in your life and the lives of others. For when others observe you, you inspire them to reach for the same alignment that you have achieved. You inspire and console them through your example. You console them because it is ever so comfortable to watch someone in alignment in action. It is comforting to watch someone who is the embodiment of Love and Kindness. It gives people hope. It gives people inspiration. It affects their vibration, even if it is just for a moment, when they watch you or even sit in your presence. For this vibrational alignment need not be expressed through words. You can simply be in a vibration of Love and fill the room with your Love simply by your mere presence. This is what you came here to experience. This is why you chose to be born. Live your purpose and be Who You Really Are, and watch how the Universe accommodates you in magical ways. This is the Spiritual Life of Pleasure that you put into your vibrational escrow as a non-physical being.

About the Author

Amélie Eden has been on her Spiritual path since she was nine years old when she began reading books from authors such as Louise Hay and Deepak Chopra. Throughout her life she has studied various religions and spiritual practices, from *A Course in Miracles* to the teachings of Abraham. She is also a self-proclaimed life-long spiritual hedonist.

Amélie has lived and studied in North America, Europe, and Asia. Throughout her life she has observed and documented ways people live, interact, and seek pleasure in various cultures around the world. One of her greatest pleasures is learning and understanding different expressions of love, spirituality, pleasure, and pleasure seeking. She describes herself as *a Spiritual Hedonista, checking out what it's like to be human.*

Amélie can often be spotted tucked away in a cozy corner of the New York Public Library, the British Library cafe, or le Jardin des Tuileries, writing about the deep mysteries of life and pleasures of living.